Fintan O'Toole is one of Ireland's most respected and contro-versial political and cultural commentators, and an acclaimed biographer and critic. His books include *White Savage*, *A Traitor's Kiss*, *Ship of Fools*, which was a number one bestseller in Ireland, and *Enough is Enough*, which was a top ten best-seller. He lives in Dublin and is assistant editor of the *Irish Times* and Leonard L. Milberg lecturer in Irish Letters at Princeton.

Further praise for *Up the Republic!*:

'At the outset of this book, O'Toole poses the essential question: "How to begin again?" This book offers no easy solutions; what is provided instead is a series of philosophical, thoughtful and nuanced reflections on what went wrong and the issues that need to be addressed to confront and learn from mistakes . . . For all there is to lament and regret in a failure to realise a working and fair republic, there is also in the book a dignified and humane in-telligence that makes it an original and constructive contribution to the literature of Ireland in crisis.' Diarmaid Ferriter, *Irish Times* by *Fintan O'Toole*

SHAKESPEARE IS HARD, BUT SO IS LIFE

A TRAITOR'S KISS

WHITE SAVAGE

SHIP OF FOOLS

ENOUGH IS ENOUGH

Up the Republic!

Towards a New Ireland

Edited by

FINTAN O'TOOLE

faber and faber

First published in 2012
by Faber and Faber Ltd
Bloomsbury House
74–77 Great Russell Street
London WC1B 3DA
This paperback edition first published in 2013

Typeset by Faber and Faber Ltd
Printed in England by CPI Group (UK) Ltd, Croydon CR0 4YY

A CIP record for this book
is available from the British Library

ISBN 978-0-571-28901-1

2 4 6 8 10 9 7 5 3 1

In memoriam
Mary Raftery 1957–2012

Contents

Contributors

ELAINE BYRNE is adjunct lecturer in the Department of Political Science at Trinity College Dublin. She initiated the *We the Citizens* project with three academic colleagues. She is the author of *Political Corruption in Ireland 1922–2010, A Crooked Harp?* www.elaine.ie

THEO DORGAN is one of Ireland's leading poets. His most recent volumes are *Greek* and *What This Earth Cost Us*. His prose works include *Time on the Ocean* and *Sailing for Home*.

TOM HICKEY is University Fellow at the School of Law in the National University of Ireland, Galway. He was a visiting research scholar at Princeton University (at the University Centre for Human Values) in 2009.

ISEULT HONOHAN is senior lecturer at the School of Politics and International Relations, University College Dublin. Her books include *Civic Republicanism* (2002) and (as editor) *Republicanism in Ireland* (2008).

DEARBHAIL MCDONALD is the Legal Editor of the *Irish Independent* and an Eisenhower Fellow. She is the author of *Bust: How the Courts Have Exposed the Rotten Heart of the Irish Economy* (2010).

CONTRIBUTORS

FINTAN O'TOOLE is assistant editor of the *Irish Times* and Leonard L. Milberg lecturer in Irish Letters at Princeton. His most recent books are *Enough is Enough* and *Ship of Fools*.

PHILIP PETTIT is Laurance S. Rockefeller University Professor of Politics and Human Values at Princeton. He is from Ballygar in County Galway. He was invited by then Spanish Prime Minister José Luis Zapatero to assess the performance of his government in the light of Pettit's 1997 *Republicanism*. His most recent books are *On the People's Terms* and *Just Freedom*.

FRED POWELL has been Professor of Social Policy and Head of the School of Applied Social Studies at University College Cork, since 1990. In 2008 he was appointed Dean of Social Science at UCC. His books include *The Politics of Civil Society: Neoliberalism or Social Left?*

Government ought to be as much open to improvement as anything which appertains to man; instead of which it has been monopolised, from age to age, by the most ignorant and vicious of the human race. Need we any other proof of their wretched management, than the excess of debts and taxes with which every nation groans, and the quarrels into which they have precipitated the world?

Thomas Paine

'Do you know what a republic is?': The Adventure and Misadventures of an Idea

FINTAN O'TOOLE

Either we shall find a way to reinforce republican politics and culture, or we shall have to resign ourselves to living in nations whose governments are controlled by the cunning and the arrogant.

Maurizio Viroli

The Twentieth Century Never Happened

In November 2011, the finance committee of parliament discussed Ireland's forthcoming budget in considerable detail. It pored over figures such as a 2 per cent rise in value added tax, a household tax of €100 and changes to capital gains tax. This was an excellent example of a republican democracy at work, with important policies being tested in public rather than merely handed down by a minister for finance like Moses bringing the tablets from the mountain top. Practices that are central to the notion of a republic – openness, accountability, the power of the executive being challenged by the elected representatives of the people – could be seen in action. It was exemplary stuff.

Meanwhile, far away, in another, less enlightened European country the finance committee of another parliament was also in session. It knew nothing of these budgetary decisions. And

why should it? Except that the parliament that was scrutinising the Irish budget was the Bundestag in Berlin and the one
that was ignorant of it was the Dáil in Dublin. In relation to
one of the most basic functions of an independent government, its annual budget, the German parliament was in the
know and the Irish parliament was in the dark.

And not just the Irish parliament – it was clear that even the
cabinet in Dublin had not yet discussed, let alone decided on,
the tax rises that were being scrutinised in the Bundestag. The
Taoiseach Enda Kenny put it plainly: 'Let me confirm something to you, the cabinet has made no decision in regard to the
budget which is on December 6th.' Yet somebody had decided
what was in the budget. When it became public that the
Bundestag had all of these details, the official line in Dublin
was that the relevant document was only a draft. But this was
obviously not so. A letter from the Irish finance minister
Michael Noonan to the European Commission, accompany-
ing the document (it was the Commission in turn that had
sent it to the Bundestag), uses the phrase 'we have decided'
before listing the measures. And in fact the details as set out
in the document were exactly those later unveiled when the
budget was presented to the Dáil.

This meant, in effect, that the Irish constitution had been
quietly suspended.

Article 28 defines the cabinet directly as 'the Government'.
It then states, with the same absolute simplicity, that 'The
executive power of the State shall, subject to the provisions of
this Constitution, be exercised by or on the authority of the
Government.' This power, moreover, must be exercised collectively: 'The Government shall meet and act as a collective
authority . . .' The standard work on the constitution, by John
Kelly, glosses this as meaning that, in relation to the statutory

functions of government, 'the valid exercise of these functions must presuppose a formal consideration and decision at a Government meeting'. There is no doubt that in relation to the 2012 budget, executive decisions were made and communicated to the EU before they were brought to the cabinet table, let alone presented to the Dáil. 'This', an unapologetic German government official told the *Irish Times*, 'is the shape of things to come.'[1]

As indeed it was. Something similar happened in late February 2012, when the Bundestag again discussed a European Commission document on the Irish economy, suggesting that further 'fiscal tightening' might be necessary. The document had not been given to the Dáil. The Taoiseach shrugged off the significance of the event in a way that suggested that this kind of thing was no longer a big deal: 'These things are unhelpful but sometimes they're overplayed.'

The German finance ministry was again patiently unapologetic, explaining that the only problem was that the document had been leaked from the parliamentary committee to which it had been given:

German law requires parliament to be involved and informed before any EFSF [European Financial Stability Facility, i.e. bailout] moneys can be disbursed. In order to fulfil this legal obligation, members of parliament require full documentation and information. The government, which has a duty to provide MPs with the information they require, very much deplores it whenever confidential information finds its way into the public domain.[2]

In fact, at around the same time, the German supreme court ruled that it was not enough that such information should be given to a small select panel of Bundestag members. Either the entire parliament or at least the 41-member budget committee would have to be convened every time a decision was to be made in relation to the use of European bailout funds. The court cited the need for 'as much parliamentary legitimisation as possible' as a reason for upholding a complaint by two opposition MPs that the panel infringed the basic right of lawmakers to decide on budgetary matters. The strong message to Ireland and to the other heavily indebted nations of the eurozone was: get used to it. The right of public, democratic scrutiny of your affairs now lies within our German democracy.

The ironies would have been too heavy-handed for good fiction. The German courts and the Bundestag were acting as such institutions ought to do in a republican democracy: insisting on openness, transparency, scrutiny and 'parliamentary legitimisation' of decisions that might affect German citizens. But they were doing so in relation to a supposed republican democracy where none of these things actually function. There could be in Ireland no openness, no advance scrutiny, no insistence on 'full documentation and information', no legitimisation of policies by elected representatives of the people. At a stroke, these parliamentary episodes demonstrated two things: (a) what republican democracies are, and (b) the fact that Ireland emphatically cannot be listed among them.

The three institutional pillars of democracy are the government, the parliament (Oireachtas) and the constitution (and hence the courts). The presentation of the budget to the Bundestag did Irish people the favour of making a nonsense of all three at once. It clarified what had been murky: that the government is no longer the executive authority, that the parliament is largely irrelevant and that the constitution has been silently suspended. It marked the death of an illusion: that Ireland is, in any meaningful sense, a republic. And it raised a poignant question: what was all that fuss and bother of the Irish twentieth century, all the thrill and trauma of a struggle for independence, actually about? It was as if the twentieth century had not happened, or rather as if a different twentieth century had unfolded in its place.

In the approach to the First World War, and in the early stages of that conflict, militant Irish nationalists asked themselves a sensible question: what if Germany wins? In 1913, in the *Fortnightly Review*, the Scots-Irish writer Sir Arthur Conan Doyle posed this three-pipe problem for Ireland, suggesting that, if Irish nationalists thought British rule was bad, they should think what the future would be like under the German Reich:

> I would venture to say one word here to my Irish fellow-countrymen of all political persuasions. If they imagine that they can stand politically or economically while Britain falls they are woefully mistaken. The British Fleet is their one shield. If it be broken, Ireland will go down. They may well throw themselves heartily into the common defence, for no sword can transfix England without the point reaching Ireland behind her.

In the *Irish Review*, a publication closely associated with two of the later signatories of the 1916 proclamation of an Irish republic, Thomas MacDonagh and Joseph Mary Plunkett, the pseudonymous 'Sean Van Vocht' replied to Doyle. He or she considered in some detail the idea that an Ireland administered, say, by Prussians would soon bitterly regret the milder manners of the Anglo-Saxon and pine for the good old days of 'doles' from Westminster. I know many Irishmen who admit that as between England and Germany they would prefer to remain in the hands of the former – on the principle that it is better to keep the devil you know than fall into the hands of a new devil. German rule, we are asked to believe, would be so bad, so stern, that under it Ireland, however much she might have suffered from England in the past, would soon yearn to be restored to the arms of her sorrowing sister.[3]

But 'Sean Van Vocht' believed that this was nonsense. What, after all, would be so bad about being ruled by Germany?

An Ireland annexed to the German Empire . . . as one of the fruits of a German victory over Great Britain, would clearly be administered as a common possession of the German people, and not as a Prussian province . . . What, then, would be the paramount object of Germany in her administration of an overseas Reichsland of such extra-ordinary geographical importance to her future as Ireland would be? Clearly not to impoverish and depress that new-won possession, but to enhance its exceeding strategic importance by vigorous and wise administration, so as to make it the main counterpoise to any possible recovery of British maritime supremacy . . . A prosperous and flour-ishing Ireland, recognising that her own interests lay with those of the new administration, would assuredly be the first and chief aim of German statesmanship. The very geographical situation of Ireland would alone ensure wise and able administration by her new rulers had Germany no other and special interest in advancing Irish well-being; for to rule from Hamburg and Berlin a remote island and a discontented people, with a highly discontented and separated Britain intervening, by methods of exploitation and centralisation, would be a task beyond the capacity of German statecraft. German effort, then, would be plainly directed to creating an Ireland satisfied with the change, and fully determined to maintain it. And it might be remembered that Germany is possibly better equipped, intellectually and educationally, for the task of developing Ireland than even 20th-century England.

Ireland, the writer imagined, would be at first like Alsace-Lorraine, annexed from France by Germany forty years earlier. The nation would feel 'alien in sentiment to her new masters to a degree that Ireland could not but be to any changes of authority imposed on her from without'. But it would learn to enjoy the benefits of wise German administration, just as Alsace-Lorraine had 'doubled in prosperity and greatly increased in population, despite . . . a rule denounced from the first as hateful. However hateful, the Prussian has proved himself an able administrator and an honest and most capable instructor. In his strong hands, Strassburg [sic] has expanded from being an ill-kept, pent-in French garrison town to a great and beautiful city.' Ireland, likewise, would benefit from 'the ablest brains in Germany, scientific, commercial and financial, no less than military and strategic' who 'would be devoted to the great task of making sure the conquest not only of an island but of the intelligence of a not unintelligent people, and by wisely developing so priceless a possession to reconcile its inhabitants, through growing prosperity and an excellent administration, to so great a change in their political environment'.

Even James Connolly, who in 1916 strung up a banner on Liberty Hall proclaiming that 'We serve neither King nor Kaiser but Ireland' was not unhappy at the thought of Ireland as 'an overseas Reichsland', a little bit of Prussia in the Atlantic. He felt that 'the German people are a highly civilised people, responsive to every progressive influence, and rapidly forging weapons of their own emancipation from native tyranny'. But even that 'tyranny' of empire seemed reasonably pleasant to his usually sceptical mind, despite the appalling realities of German colonialism in Namibia:

> The German Empire is a homogeneous Empire of self-governing peoples; the British Empire is a heterogeneous collection in which a very small number of self-governing communities connive at the subjugation, by force, of a vast number of despotically ruled subject populations. We do not wish to be ruled by either empire, but we certainly believe that the first named contains in germ more of the possibilities of freedom and civilisation than the latter.[4]

By 1916, of course, the Germans had become, in the words of the proclamation read out by Patrick Pearse in the same year, 'our gallant allies in Europe' – the Irish republic would implicitly be born under the wing of the German imperial eagle.

There is, now, no German empire. Germany did not win the war, nor the next one. And it would be hysterical to suggest, as some English eurosceptics do, that the European Union is now effectively a German Reich under another guise. Germany is a fine and admirable democracy, not a militaristic Prussian autocracy. Ireland has not been annexed to anybody's empire – it used its independence to destroy its own sovereignty. But there is none the less an inescapable reality that the centre of governance that was moved from London to Dublin in 1922 has now moved again to Berlin and to Frankfurt, home of the European Central Bank, which is unquestionably the single most powerful institution in Irish public life.

This happened because, in the banking crisis that erupted in 2008, the Irish government did exactly as it was told by the ECB. Brian Cowen, who was Taoiseach at the time, has since made it plain that he was only following orders when he made the catastrophic decision to guarantee all of the debts of the Irish banks, including the extravagantly delinquent Anglo Irish Bank:

> At no stage during the crisis would the European authorities, especially the European Central Bank, have countenanced the dishonouring of senior bank bonds. The euro-area policy of 'No bank failures and no burning of senior bank creditors' has been a constant during the crisis. And as a member of the euro area, Ireland must play by the rules.[5]

There were in fact no such 'rules' – at no point did the Irish parliament ever debate, let alone accede to, the idea of a legal requirement to nationalise private debt at the cost of destroying its own public finances, losing its capacity to borrow on international markets and being forced to give up its sovereignty in return for a so-called bailout by the same people who had pushed the country into beggary.

This, indeed, is a perfect example of what writers in the classical tradition of republicanism defined as tyranny: the imposition on a people of laws it had not itself made or consented to. In this sense, Irish sovereignty was not lost in the dramatic moment when officials from the European Commission, the ECB and the International Monetary Fund arrived in Dublin to impose conditions in return for money. It was lost when an Irish government was bullied or persuaded to follow 'rules' that had no basis in law or democracy, even when doing so had dire long-term consequences for its own citizens.

Ireland's current status, resulting from those decisions, is not unlike the kind of Home Rule that was supposed to come into force in 1914: local autonomy without fiscal or budgetary control. Except that such control does not reside in England but in Germany. This was, for the revolutionaries of 1916, not their desired outcome, but an acceptable second best. And it is now, in a highly qualified but none the less grotesque sense, the terminus of the journey they initiated. The country is now actually rather like the 'self-governing' entity under German hegemony that Connolly thought it might be if the outcome of the First World War had been different. In a strange and unexpected way, the alternative future that radical Irish nationalists imagined at that time has become the one in which their political descendants actually live.

Forgetting the Republic

There is, in the approach to the centenary of the 1916 Rising, a concern with how the declaration of the republic is to be remembered and commemorated. But in fact what characterises the Irish republic is much more the act of forgetting it. At least three times, the republic has been declared and then allowed to slip from the national consciousness.

Amnesia, as the French thinker Ernest Renan suggested in 1882, is essential to the foundation of nations. 'Forgetfulness, and I shall even say historical error, form an essential factor in the creation of a nation.' What must be forgotten? The 'deeds of violence that have taken place at the commencement of all political formations . . . Unity is ever achieved by brutality.' A nation is also based on a common forgetting of its inevitably mixed ethnic origins. 'But the essence of a nation is that all its individual members should have many things in common; and also that all of them should hold many things in oblivion . . . It is good for all to know how to forget.'[6]

The Irish republic, though, is not quite like this. It is steeped in forgetting but in a most peculiar way. Renan's amnesia is a creative act – nations found themselves on acts of forgetting. But the Irish republic goes much further – it forgets its own foundation, time and again. And what it shoves to the back of its mind is not the circumstance of its creation but its own existence.

There is something decidedly odd about the 1916 proclamation. Its signatories 'hereby proclaim the Irish Republic as a Sovereign Independent State, and we pledge our lives and the lives of our comrades in arms to the cause of its freedom, of its welfare, and of its exaltation among the nations'. The authors seem to forget that the organisation to which they belong, the Irish Republican Brotherhood, had long since declared this Irish republic as an existing entity. Logically, the 1916 proclamation should have been a restatement or a rededication, not a founding act at all.

For, almost half a century earlier, in 1867, the IRB issued an apparently definitive declaration: 'Herewith we proclaim the Irish Republic.' That this first proclamation is remembered only by historians and never referred to in public discourse is in itself unremarkable. What is remarkable is that the IRB seems to have wilfully dis-remembered it. Perhaps it was felt to be more dramatically potent to begin again, to mark the Easter Rising as a self-conscious point of origin. Perhaps a grand proclamation is easier to kill and die for than an act of memory and recapitulation.

Or perhaps the first declaration of the Irish republic was a little uncomfortable in its social radicalism and open secularism. The 1867 proclamation has none of the religious and mystical language of the 1916 proclamation. God, invoked twice in 1916, was not imagined as an honorary citizen of the 1867 republic – he or she is entirely absent. Ireland is not invoked as an abstract entity, summoning 'her children to her flag'. The 1867 references to the country are concrete: 'the soil of Ireland'; 'the Irish people'. On the other hand, the 1867 proclamation does mention certain things absent in 1916: a republican form of government (as against both 'oligarchy' and 'the curse of Monarchical Government'); economic injustice ('the oppression of labour'); and economic equality ('we aim at founding a Republic based on universal suffrage, which shall secure to all the intrinsic value of their labour').

Even more uncomfortably, the 1867 proclamation resists ideas of either religious or ethnic solidarity as the basis for the Irish republic. It is explicitly secular: 'We declare, also, in favour of absolute liberty of conscience, and complete separation of Church and State.' And it does not create a simple opposition of 'Irish' to 'English'. It declares war on 'aristocratic locusts, whether English or Irish, who have eaten the verdure of our fields'. On the other hand, it imagines, however fancifully, a common cause with the English working class: 'As for you, workmen of England, it is not only your hearts we wish, but your arms.'

This putative Irish republic had to be forgotten in 1916, even though the leaders of the Rising had in fact sworn oaths of allegiance to it. Strikingly, though, this is not the only act of wilful amnesia in the 1916 proclamation. It explicitly calls to mind the idea of oblivion, declaring the new republic to be 'oblivious of the differences carefully fostered by an alien Government, which have divided a minority from the majority in the past'. The desired import is that 'differences' – the profound division between largely Catholic nationalism and largely Protestant unionism that had just brought the island to the brink of civil war – *should* be forgotten. But the effect is, rather, that they *have* been forgotten. The proclamation is in this sense too an act of forgetting – its whole gesture of declaring a republic relies on the throwing of a mental cordon sanitaire around Unionism. It is delicately and euphemistically broached, but only in order to be immediately dismissed from consciousness. 'Oblivious' here is a well-chosen word.

In any event, the 1916 republic was itself quickly forgotten. It was, in part, overtaken by partition. But it was also treated with little respect by its own heirs – the politicians who came to power in the southern Free State. In 1919, the first Dáil attempted to formulate in concrete terms what the republic might actually mean. That meaning, it agreed, would have to centre on the idea of social equality – the republic would have to belong equally to all its citizens. In introducing the Democratic Programme which the Dáil adopted, Richard Mulcahy said, 'A nation cannot be fully free in which even a small section of its people have not freedom. A nation cannot be said fully to live in spirit, or materially, while there is denied to any section of its people a share of the wealth and the riches that God bestowed around them.' Accordingly, the Democratic Programme explicitly announced that the 1916 proclamation meant that 'all right to private property must be subordinated to the public right and welfare'. It defined the republic as one whose first duty would be to the welfare of children, which would create 'a sympathetic native scheme for the care of the Nation's aged and infirm, who shall not be regarded as a burden, but rather entitled to the Nation's gratitude and consideration'; and which would create an effective public healthcare system.[7]

All of this was adopted unanimously and without debate – a sign not that it represented the serious commitment of the Dáil but in fact that it did not. In Irish political culture, it is a safe bet that anything that is unanimous is a mere gesture. The first Dáil actually did something extraordinary: it teased out what the real meaning of the republic declared in 1916 would be and then promptly forgot all about it. Within four months, by April 1919, Eamon de Valera announced that the implementation of the Democratic Programme would have to be postponed. Kevin O'Higgins, one of the most influential figures in the early years of the Free State, later dismissed the Democratic Programme as 'mostly poetry'. It was, in the event, not merely consigned to oblivion but actively traduced: child welfare, for example, was monumentally abused.

But did the 1916 republic ever exist in any corporeal form? In 1935, the senior surviving leader of the Rising, Eamon de Valera, declared that 'they were not going to declare a republic during this period of office'.[8] Yet, by 1937, he was declaring that his new constitution gave Ireland 'all the symbols and institutions of a Republic except the title'. But yet again in 1937, he declared that 'the unity of Ireland under a new Constitution is far more desirable for him than any declaration of a republic for the truncated country'.[9] Even the arch-republican could not say whether Ireland was a republic or not.

And so the republic, twice forgotten, was declared all over again. The Irish republic was inaugurated, this time by an

Irish government, on Easter Monday, 18 April 1949, with a ceremony at the General Post Office in Dublin. The day and place were chosen to resonate with the declaration of the republic at the same spot thirty-three years earlier. But the irony of the gesture seems to have escaped the government: it was proclaiming again the republic that had been proclaimed in 1916 by those who believed it had already been proclaimed in 1867. This was a republic so good they proclaimed it thrice. Or, perhaps, one so nebulous that, however often it was declared, it remained always intangible and out of reach.

And this third declaration of the republic was itself effectively being forgotten even as it was being declared. It generated little public excitement: 'It was noted that the ceremonies chiefly involved politicians and the military. The inauguration of a republic and the ceremonies associated with it failed to engage the enthusiastic support of the population in general.[10] This is unsurprising. The declaration had been made suddenly and without prior discussion in the Dáil or in public: the citizens of this new republic learned of it in news from Canada, where it was announced by the Taoiseach, John A. Costello.

In fact, the great day of the third inauguration of the republic had elements of high comedy. It provided an Irish twist on Karl Marx: the republic was declared the second time (in 1916) as tragedy and the third (in 1949) as farce. De Valera refused to attend, ostentatiously spending the day at Arbour Hill 'praying for the men of 1916'. (Considering the men of 1916 had long since been canonised, it is not clear why they needed his prayers.) A barman – that source of infallible popular wisdom – commented, 'Sure, it's all politics. Costello and his crowd have wiped Dev's eye and now Dev is trying to get his own back on them.'[11] The Irish Grand National at Fairyhouse drew larger crowds than the birth of the republic.

Brian Inglis in the *Irish Times* reported:

There was very little real warmth in the cheering, very
little real gaiety in the atmosphere. There were loud
cheers, but they were the cheers of people just tired of
standing there, waiting for something to happen. There
were gay crowds, but they were the usual, idle, bank
holiday crowds, prepared to watch any free show until
such time as the cinemas opened their doors, and they
could settle down in earnest to the business of enjoying
the holiday.

There was even trouble getting the new republic's tricolour
of green, white and orange right:

There appears to be some doubt in the public mind, or
in the minds of the manufacturers of flags, as to what
exactly constitutes the national flag of the Republic.
Apart from the normal variations in the hue – primrose
yellow to blood orange – quite a number of the small
hand flags had the orange instead of the green next to
the staff, and I saw one small girl waving a tricolour on
which the green, white and orange stripes had been
arranged horizontally instead of vertically.

Souvenir sellers were having a hard time. They shouted 'get
your Republican colours . . . get your colours for the Republic' in the same tone, Inglis noted, as they usually roared 'get
your colours for the match'. But to little avail. The price of
souvenirs – small Irish flags with gold tassels and pictures of
Wolfe Tone or the GPO – started at sixpence. By the time
the military parade got under way, the price was down to

twopence, and even before it ended they were being knocked down for a penny.[12]

Souvenirs, after all, are meant to stir memories. The crowd may have sensed that this republic, too, would be forgotten. In reality, the declaration of a republic in 1949 changed nothing much. Ireland left the British Commonwealth and this negative act was the only meaning the new republic ever had. Asked by the London editor of the *Irish Times* whether the Republic of Ireland Act marked a step forward in Ireland's development, a sceptical George Bernard Shaw replied, 'Ask me five years hence. If the terrible vital statistics improve to a civilised level, then our steps will have been steps forward. If not, there will be nothing for us but the ancient prescription of the submergence of the island for ten minutes in the Irish Sea.'

Shaw's scepticism was entirely justified. The new republic changed little – not even the name of the state, which remained simply Ireland. The term 'Republic of Ireland' was declared to be 'the description of the State' – not its name. The Republic of Ireland Act is in fact a desultory piece of legislation, containing five sentences totalling 96 words. It could be so short because it had nothing to say, nothing to bring into effect. Everything carried on exactly as before. The vital statistics of the population – life expectancy, health status, poverty, levels of education – did not improve, unless, of course, people left for other countries, as they did in their droves in the decade after the new republic was inaugurated.

This, in itself, surely says something about the idea of an Irish republic. If you can declare it in 96 words that have no consequence, it is only because you have become used to forgetting it. It is an airy, insubstantial thing.

The Republic of Vague

One of the things that makes 'the republic' a slippery concept is the existence of two quite separate traditions of republicanism. Philip Pettit has drawn a sharp distinction between them. The first tradition is the one that emerged from classical Roman thought ('what affects all must be decided by all'), by way of the Italian Renaissance. It took shape in Florence, Venice and the other city states, and went on to underpin the overthrow of monarchs in Poland, Holland and England in the seventeenth and eighteenth centuries. It enormously influenced the American Revolution and partly (but only partly) shaped the French.

This stream of thought had three basic elements. First, freedom should be understood as the condition, in Pettit's formulation, of 'not having to live under the potentially harmful power of another' person: in other words, 'non-domination'. The state's job is not merely to uphold this freedom but – crucially – to uphold it equally for all citizens.

This makes the idea of republican freedom very different from liberal and neoliberal definitions of 'freedom', which include the freedom to exploit and control others. 'Non-domination' is not the same thing as 'non-interference'. Non-domination actually requires radical state interference at times: to uphold the equal rights of women, for example, or to prevent employers from exploiting their dominance over their workers, or to stop banks from engaging in behaviour that will impose crushing debts on citizens. It may even require at times a degree of compulsion: paying taxes, for example, is a duty because the state has to have the resources to provide those things that are necessary for everyone to live with dignity. 'The continual whine of lamenting the burden of taxes . . .', says the great republican Thomas Paine, 'is inconsistent with the sense and spirit of a republic.'[13]

Classical republicanism is concerned, in a way that liberalism is not, with the cost to human dignity of being in a state of dependence on the whims of others. As Maurizio Viroli puts it:

> Liberal liberty aims to protect individuals only from interferences, from actions interfering with their freedom of choice; republican liberty aims to emancipate them from the conditions of dependence. What worries a liberal is having anyone's freedom of action dominated or controlled; a republican worries about this but worries even more about the dispiritedness that affects men and women who live dependent lives.[14]

In this sense, republicanism is very much at odds with the currently dominant idea that good societies can be shaped by governments whose main concern is simply not to interfere with the functioning of markets. It is an ideal of freedom – but freedom defined much more richly than the liberty that right-wing orthodoxy proclaims as its central principle.

Republicanism requires a strong state, therefore, but it also seeks to limit and contest the power of the state. Hence the second and third elements of classical republican thinking. The second principle holds that government should be 'mixed', its various powers and functions broken up among different and independent bodies to ensure that no one could exercise unaccountable power. Third, it is up to citizens, individually and collectively, to keep the republic on its toes, in Pettit's phrase to 'track and contest public policies and initiatives'. Crudely, in a republic, nobody gets to dominate anybody else, nobody gets unaccountable power and citizens have a duty to be obstreperous. The aim of all of this is to strike a balance: the state should be strong enough to stop one citizen from bullying another, but not so strong that it itself becomes the bully.

These ideals were, historically, limited in their application. The citizens who made up the early republican states were male property owners. Slaves, women, the poor and colonial subjects were generally beyond its pale. Other groups – non-whites, indigenous peoples, Jews, Catholics and so on – might or might not be allowed into the republic. Republics often acted in practice as guarantors of non-domination for their members but as instruments of domination towards others. But this does not mean that the principles themselves are to be despised. On the contrary, the very fact that privileged groups have hoarded them for themselves and kept them from others suggests that they are well worth possessing. Their point, after all, is human dignity, the ideal, in Pettit's words, of 'being sufficiently empowered to stand on equal terms with others, as a citizen among citizens . . . [to] be able to walk tall, live without shame or indignity, and look one another in the eye without any reason for fear or deference'.

There is, though, another, radically different, tradition of republicanism. It is the tradition of Rousseau, crucially influential on the French Revolution and on much Continental European thinking since. It accepts and indeed insists on the first principle of the other tradition: that citizens should be free of domination by others. But it rejects the other two: the ideas of mixed government and of the obstreperous citizenry. Instead of the idea that power should be deliberately divided, the Rousseau tradition argues for the notion of a single, sovereign popular will: 'the People' effectively taking the place

of the king in a monarchy. A popular assembly should decide
the 'general will', which then becomes absolute law. There is
no room in the general will for different parts of government
holding each other in check. This would 'turn the Sovereign
into a being that is fantastical and formed of disparate parts'.
And it follows also that there is no room for obstreperous
citizens. Once the 'general will' has been expressed by the
assembly, it must be accepted and obeyed – otherwise it would
not be general. As Pettit characterises this position:

> Far from every law being a fair target for civic critique
> and challenge, each comes draped in an authority and
> majesty that brooks no individual opposition. Having
> been party to the creation of the popular sovereign no
> one as an individual retains the right of contesting the
> decisions of the collectivity, even if those decisions were
> ones that the person argued against in assembly.

In this view, a republic is essentially the right to participate in
decision-making. Once decisions have been made, the entire
force of the state and of the citizens collectively is assumed to
be behind them.

The immediate question that faces us here is not which of
these republican traditions is best but which of them Ireland
has followed. Is the republic, as it has taken shape in nine-
teenth- and twentieth-century politics, of the first (let's call it
Renaissance) kind? Or is it of the Rousseau variety? The
answer, as with so much in Irish culture, is both and neither.
The Irish republic has strong elements of both traditions but
has never functioned as a coherent expression of either. There
are good historical reasons for this – Irish republicanism
being halfway between the American and French Revolutions

– but the result is a blurry, and therefore largely impotent, concept.

In some ways, the Irish republic has been expressed in terms that Rousseau would recognise. In the way Rousseau's ideas are developed through European nationalism, 'the people or community gets to be sacralized, as it assumes the role of the popular, incontestable sovereign, incapable of doing wrong to its own members'. There is a very strong tradition of imagining Ireland in this way, as a sacred, incontestable and sovereign entity who commands the allegiance of her children. In the opening paragraph of the 1916 proclamation: 'Ireland, through us, summons her children . . .' 'Ireland' is imagined as a single, sacred and sovereign force, the embodiment of the popular or general will.

But there is a refinement. At least in Rousseau, the general will is decided by a deliberative assembly of the people before it becomes sacred and commanding. But the conditions of Ireland – first British rule, then partition – mean that this great democratic assembly has never happened, except, perhaps, as a result of the 1918 general election when the whole island voted at the same time. So who is to decide the general will in the meantime? A vanguard or elite that has distinguished itself by the absolute nature of its commitment to Ireland. It will act, often violently, in the certain knowledge that it is expressing the general will and that the great assembly, whenever it becomes possible, will retrospectively endorse those actions. This is an extreme version of Rousseau – sacred, unified and implacable sovereignty but without the initial act of democratic deliberation.

This is what those who are habitually referred to, even now, as 'republicans' – members of the IRA or one of its many offshoots – believe. But the idea has also had a milder expression in the less fanatical politics of the real Irish state. The idea of Ireland as a single, sovereign entity that is sacred and therefore not to be argued with lies behind an authoritarian streak in Irish politics. Here, the 'general will' becomes the 'national interest' – a concept that always happens to coincide with the specific interests of a ruling party and/or of a powerful section of society. (It was in the 'national interest' that all private banking debts be rendered public, therefore public discussion or scrutiny was deemed irrelevant at best, impertinent at worst.) In vulgar terms, the appeal is made to 'pull on the green jersey' – to obey the summons of 'Ireland' without further discussion. The idea of accountability implicit in mixed government is ditched. And the citizenry's duty to be obstreperous is annulled. On the contrary, its duty is to be stoical, taciturn and 'resilient'.

This strain of republicanism has been expressed in Irish politics chiefly through the historic dominance of an organisation that saw itself, quite explicitly, as the expression of the 'general will'. Fianna Fáil, The Republican Party (to give it its full official title) refused to see itself as one political party among others and therefore as a group of citizens engaged in the open contest of democracy. Its self-image is, rather, that of a 'national movement'. This is the primary idea in its constitution which begins 'Fianna Fáil is a National Movement' and then dictates that 'the Movement shall be organised and known as Fianna Fáil, The Republican Party'.

The suggestion here is that of a relationship similar to that of God the Father to God the Son. On earth, God the Son takes a physical, corporeal, human form: Fianna Fáil. But this physical and temporal form is just a manifestation of something entirely beyond our human ken, the national movement. And, of course, inherent in this mystical politics is the notion that the national movement really is the nation and that disloyalty to the party is really a form of treachery. Even after its humiliation in the 2011 general election, the party's self-description continues to state baldly, 'Fianna Fáil represents the mainstream of Irish life.' To be outside a party that 80 per cent of Irish people do not support is thus to be outside the Irish mainstream, to be marginal and inauthentic.

But this idea could be, and was, pushed even further. The party connected itself rhetorically to the French Revolution, defining its republicanism as a mixture of nationalism and internationalism. 'Republican', it says, 'stands both for the unity of the island and a commitment to the historic principles of European republican philosophy, namely liberty, equality and fraternity.' But just as the 'general will' in the French Revolution found its ultimate expression in Napoleonic triumphalism, Fianna Fáil inevitably produced its own mini-Napoleon, Charles Haughey. Haughey (who was privately obsessed with Napoleon) gave his grandiose collection of speeches the Rousseauesque title 'The Spirit of the Nation'. The logic was impeccable: if the party was really the mere physical manifestation of the nation, its leader must represent in himself the embodiment of the general will, the nation's abiding spirit. (And bribes to the leader were not bribes but votive offerings, sacrifices to the nation itself.)

Ludicrous as all of this was and is, it is well to remember that the claim that Fianna Fáil represented 'the mainstream of Irish life' was perfectly tenable for seventy-five years. It had – and may still have – a powerful hold. There are, therefore, strong elements of the Rousseau tradition of republicanism in Irish political culture.

But only elements. For at the same time, Irish republicanism, in the institutional form it has taken in the southern state, draws heavily on the other, Renaissance, tradition. It accepts, at least in theory, the two principles that Rousseau rejects. It has a classic mixed government, with power divided among the executive, the judiciary and the parliament. It is a society of laws: courts can and do overrule the actions of the government when they impinge on the rights of citizens. And it does acknowledge at least the basic foundations of active, vigilant citizenship – rights to freedom of expression and assembly, for example.

In practice, however, the Irish state has been very far from the conception of a classical republic. It can be tested against the three basic components of that tradition and found starkly wanting:

Non-domination

For most of its history, the state failed miserably in the basic task of ensuring that citizens were free from subjection to the arbitrary will of others. It allowed the institutional Catholic Church (as opposed to Catholics themselves) to exercise unaccountable and secretive power in key areas of the public and private lives of citizens, from access to contraception to basic public services such as healthcare and education. The state also actively colluded in grotesque systems of arbitrary power, such as industrial schools, Magdalene Homes and mental hospitals – incarcerating without trial a higher proportion of its citizens than the Soviet Union did.

More recently, the state itself has been dominated by private interests. Corruption allowed wealthy citizens to purchase public policy, to the detriment of the majority of their fellow citizens. The skewing of the planning process for the capital city over two decades is just one example. And even when corruption was not at play, specific interest groups – the banks being an obvious example – acquired a position of complete (and in the event, disastrous) dominance over key areas of public policy.

Mixed Government

In principle, the Irish state was structured around a classic division of power, with the idea that the government, the courts and the parliament would each keep the others in check. In practice, the division of power has been at best partial. It is broadly true that courts have acted as a check on government, though even this has to be qualified by three important factors. One is that access to the courts has been unequal, with some citizens having no practical way to vindicate their rights. The second is that the law itself has been unequally applied, with some categories of intensely destructive crime (corruption, fraud, tax evasion) enjoying large-scale impunity and others (generally those committed by the denizens of the underclass) being harshly punished. Thirdly, the independence of the judiciary from the government it is supposed to check is severely limited: judges depend on government for appointment and there is a strong connection between judicial appointments and membership of the party in power.

But if the judicial and legal side of the exercise of power has been imperfect, the parliamentary side has been virtually non-existent. Parliament, in general, does not initiate legislation; it passes it. Scrutiny of legislation is often extremely minimal. The accountability of ministers is barely existent, and that of senior civil servants (who in effect make many key decisions) is virtually non-existent. This key aspect of republican tradition amounts, in the Irish case, to little more than a constitutional fiction.

Obstreperous Citizens

The third plank of the Renaissance republican tradition is the idea that citizens, individually and collectively, have both the right and the duty to be critically engaged with everything the state is doing on their behalf. It is somewhat ironic that the most famous formulation of this idea is Irish: John Philpot Curran, on his election as Lord Mayor of Dublin in 1790 said that the 'condition upon which God hath given liberty to man is eternal vigilance' (subsequently quoted as 'the price of liberty is eternal vigilance' and widely misattributed to Thomas Jefferson). It would be an exaggeration to say that this vigilant citizenry has been absent from the Irish republic. But its presence has been limited and ineffective.

The limitations are fourfold. First, the political system (and the wider political culture) has encouraged Irish people to think of themselves not as citizens but as clients. Voting is a deal: I get you a state or local-government service and you pay me with your vote. The model is closer to the logic of the marketplace than to that of an active democracy. Second, the arena in which it should be easiest for citizens to acquire the habit of exercising their right to a voice and their responsibility to make good choices – local democracy – is extraordinarily weak by international standards.

Third, the basic precondition for an engaged citizenship is information. Citizens need to know what it is they're supposed to be vigilant about. The Irish republic has an extremely poor record of transparency and openness. For much of the history of the state, free discussion was heavily discouraged by the power of the institutional Church, its 'moral monopoly' on opinions on a range of issues, and by active censorship. More recently, experiments with freedom of state information in the 1990s were actively and deliberately rolled back. The capacity of citizens to know what the state is doing remains extremely limited. The blanket guarantee given to Irish banks in 2008 is a prime example – at no point was the public ever given the most basic information about its cost until it was far too late.

Lastly and more nebulously, Ireland has a very strong cultural orientation towards the acceptance of orthodoxies and the marginalisation or co-option of dissent. The very weak role of ideology in the political culture (with the two main parties being effectively identical in almost every area of policy) has discouraged the notion that a clash of ideas is healthy. The intimate nature of the society has encouraged an ideal of consensus. The heavy concentration of ownership, especially in the print media, has limited the scope for genuine debate. Those in power have been very adept at buying off useful dissidents when they can and closing them down when they must. And Irish culture is heavily shaped by fatalism and a sense of powerlessness. Its instinct is to adapt to circumstances rather than to change them. All of these factors have greatly weakened the idea of a powerful, engaged citizenry that is so central to classical republicanism.

Ireland has thus had elements of both the competing traditions of republicanism, without fully engaging with either of them. It has been, at best, a blurry republic, in which the two traditions have tended to cancel each other out. The vagueness has not been entirely disadvantageous. It is a reasonable guess that if one of the traditions were to have clarified itself sufficiently to have become entirely dominant, it would not have been the more open, sceptical and engaged Renaissance one. That tradition might have been relatively weak, but it was strong enough to act as a barrier to the complete triumph of the 'general will'. It was able to resist the pull of an ethnic, mystical, authoritarian republicanism which the Provisional IRA tried to mobilise between the 1960s and the 1990s. And though it failed to stop Haughey from doing immense harm to the body politic, it did at least put limits on the extent of his power.

A blurry republicanism with some saving graces is, however, still too slippery and uncertain to achieve what a republican ethic is supposed to: to create and sustain a political community that belongs equally to all its members and has their common good as its purpose. And arguably one of the reasons that never happened is that there has never been a time when Irish people have been offered the hard bargain that a republic implies: an offer of freedom and dignity that demands in return a collective commitment to the maintenance of the conditions that make those things available to all.

Terms and Conditions Apply

During the French Revolution of 1848, an angry crowd stormed the Hôtel de Ville in Paris where the provisional government was sitting. They demanded to see its head, the poet Alphonse de Lamartine.

'We have upset the monarchy, let Lamartine tell us do they mean to give us the republic?'

'Who said republic?' asked Lamartine.

'All!'

'Do you know what you are asking? Do you know what a republic means?'

'Tell us.'

'The republic, do you know that it is the government of the

reason of all men? Do you think you are prepared to be rulers of yourselves, and to have no other masters than your own reason?'

'Yes!'

'The republic, do you know that it is the government of justice? Are you just enough to do right even to your enemies?'

'Yes!'

'Are you virtuous enough to forbear vengeance, proscriptions, and blood, which dishonoured the former republic?'

'Yes, yes!'

'You will? You are? You swear it? You call Heaven to witness it?'

A thunder of affirmation followed.

'Well, then,' said Lamartine, 'you shall be a republic, if you are as worthy to keep it as you have been to conquer it. But understand, we must not begin the republic by injustice: we have no business to steal a republic, we can only declare our wish in the name of the people of Paris. It is a glorious initiative; but the thirty millions of men who compose the French people are not here: they have a right to be consulted. The forms of our institutions shall be decided by the universal suffrage of the French people: it is the only basis of a national republic.'

'Yes,' cried the crowd. 'It is just. Paris is the head, but it is not France. The head has no right to oppress the members. Vive la République!'[15]

The story has obviously been shaped as a heroic epic, but it is suggestive none the less. It is striking that Lamartine says, not 'you shall *have* a republic', but 'you shall *be* a republic'. A republic is not something people are given but something they choose to become. The choice is conscious, deliberate and difficult. And it is tested. There is this moment in French

30

history when the demand for a republic is met with three key questions. Do you know what it is? Are you ready to take on the responsibilities of self-rule? And do you accept that terms and conditions apply, that your own anger and passion are not enough but must be qualified by reason, justice and democratic consent? At least in this epic myth, the French crowd is given the opportunity to answer 'yes' or 'no'.

These questions have never actually been asked of the Irish people, even in a romantic myth. The Irish have no narrative of republican call and response; they have only the call, the 'summons' of the 1916 proclamation. Republics have been declared for them: in 1867 and 1916 by secretive revolutionary vanguards and in 1948 by a Taoiseach on a trip to Canada. Each time, the republic has come as a surprise to its putative citizens. It has been easily forgotten because it was easily invented. Lamartine's hard question – Do you think you are prepared to be rulers of yourselves? – has never been truly probed.

That question is about one of the basic ideas that has always been present in republican thinking: civic virtue, defined as the 'willingness and capacity [of citizens] to serve the common good'. Citizens have to be 'as worthy to keep' a republic as they are to get it in the first place. A republic demands constant care. In 1944, just before he was executed at the age of nineteen by a fascist firing squad, the Italian resistance fighter Giacomo Ulivi wrote of the republic he was willing to die for that 'we need to take direct, personal care of it'.[16]

It is obvious that the Irish people as a whole have taken spectacularly bad care of their republic. If it was a child, the social workers would have come for it long ago, for it has shown terrible signs of abuse and neglect. They have not demanded accountability of their leaders. They have continued to elect politicians they know to have abused power. They voted in large numbers for Haughey, who openly flaunted extreme wealth after a lifetime in public office. They chose to suspend their disbelief in the ridiculous lies spun by Haughey's protégé Bertie Ahern to explain large sums of cash for which he could not account. They displayed what the report of the Mahon Tribunal into the perversion of the planning process calls 'general apathy' towards the existence of 'systemic and endemic' corruption.

To return to Ernest Renan, he argued that a nation is made up of two things: the past and the present. A nation 'implies a past; but it is summed up in the present by a tangible fact – consent, the clearly expressed desire to live a common life'. The same might more accurately be said of republics. Ireland is very strong on the first aspect, the past. But is very weak on the present. It has never manifested 'the clearly expressed desire to live a common life'. But then the citizens have never really been asked to express clearly their commitment to a republic.

Talk of civic virtue conjures up unfortunate images of idealised Romans dressed in togas or of fanatical Robespierres sharpening their own incorruptibility to such a keen edge that it can cut off the heads of the unworthy. In fact, it is a much simpler and less po-faced idea: 'Civic virtue is not a martial, heroic and austere virtue, but a civilised, ordinary tolerant one.'[17] It is not even at odds with the idea that is often counterpoised against it: self-interest. It simply asks that self-interest be enlightened. It suggests that the 'self' in which we are interested is not an isolated, robotic machine for calculating immediate advantage, but a nexus of connections to family, to place and nature, to community, to society, to the imaginary but potent entity we call a nation. It entails a belief that human beings take personal pleasure in trust and decency and collective achievement. It imagines the self to include both a moral sense that finds satisfaction in justice and an aesthetic sense that is repelled by the chaos, disorder and obscenity of a society that pits all against all and is gratified by balance and decency.

It would be ridiculous to suggest that Irish people lack these qualities. There is no genetic flaw that makes the Irish less inclined to public virtue than other people. On the contrary, it is the very strong sense of collective identity, the obvious hunger for a sense of common purpose and the evidence of altruistic commitment at both the local and international levels that make the inability of these qualities to manifest themselves at the level of a national republic so extraordinary.

There are many factors at work and the biggest ones are obvious. Machine politics with a clientilistic ethic were already well established, both at home and in the wider culture of the Irish diaspora, before the foundation of the state. The strongest moral and philosophical influence on society – institutional Catholicism – was overwhelmingly concerned with ideas of private virtue (the control of sexuality in particular), largely to the exclusion of civic virtue. Cities – the arenas in which classical republicanism was incubated – were few and small. Conversely, an intense sense of and attachment to the local, which developed in response to the remoteness of power when Ireland was ruled from London, worked against identification with national politics: given a choice between a politician who would bring short-term benefits to the locality but harm the national body politic and one who would promise little for the locality but benefit the country as a whole, Irish voters would almost always choose the former.

Mass emigration continually undermined the idea of a 'we' on which a republican culture is based. The 'desire to live a common life' might have been present, but it was literally diffused. The 'common life' that binds together a culture shaped by mass emigration is a life of the imagination – memory, nostalgia, the myths of identity – but not of daily reality. It is, in Renan's terms, a life of the past but not of the present.

Those who stayed at home, meanwhile, were caught in a largely static economy in which the idea of mutual benefit – an idea essential to republicanism – was not at all obvious. In a static world, everything is a zero-sum game. There is only so much of everything – money, land, prestige, education – so everything you get is something I'm not getting. Thus the inbred ethic of begrudgery so well caught by Joe Lee:

> The Irish carry from their mother's womb not so much a
> fanatic heart as a begrudger one. The begrudger mentality
> did derive fairly rationally from a mercantilist concept of
> the size of the status cake. The size of that cake was more
> or less fixed in more or less static communities and in
> small institutions. In a stunted society, one man's gain
> did tend to be another man's loss. Winners could flourish
> only at the expense of losers. Status depended not only
> on rising oneself but on preventing others from rising. For
> many, keeping the other fellow down presented the surest
> defence of their own position.[18]

One of the preconditions of a republic – that one's status depends on one's willingness to help others to rise – was not merely absent but turned on its head.

Another aspect of this culture was fatalism. Generations of suffering and poverty bred a habit of being grateful for small mercies. The German novelist Heinrich Böll, who lived much of the time on Achill island, wrote in 1957:

34

When something happens to you in Germany, when you miss a train, break a leg, go bankrupt, we say: It couldn't have been any worse; whatever happens is always the worst. With the Irish it is almost the opposite: if you break a leg, miss a train, go bankrupt, they say: it could be worse; instead of a leg you might have broken your neck, instead of a train you might have missed Heaven . . . Whatever happens is never the worst; on the contrary, what's worst never happens: if your revered and beloved grandmother dies, your revered and beloved grandfather might have died too . . . 'It could be worse' is one of the most common turns of speech, probably because only too often things are pretty bad and what's worse offers the consolation of being relative.[19]

There is an element of stereotype in this, of course, but also a large element of truth: even in the years of prosperity, 'Could be worse' remained a standard response to the question 'How are you?'

Beyond these obvious forces, there is the role of nationalism. There is no necessary contradiction between republicanism and nationalism. An ethnic or sectarian nationalism that insists on a homogeneous identity as the condition of full citizenship is certainly incompatible with classical republicanism. Ireland has obvious experience of that brand of identity. But there are other kinds of civic, pluralist nationalism that can sit perfectly well with the existence of a republic. In principle at least, Irish nationalism and a genuine Irish republicanism might have made comfortable bedfellows. But two aspects of nationalism – one general and one highly specific – made this marriage impossible.

The general question relates to the notion at the heart of civic virtue – that a republic can't just be declared, it has to be maintained as a daily concern of all of its citizens: 'We need to take direct, personal care of it.' A republic can be gained, but it can also be lost: it can be hijacked by oligarchies or interest groups or it can slowly corrode through neglect or corruption. But this is absolutely not true of a nation in the way nationalism imagines it. In nationalist thinking, the nation is always there. It was created by god or nature or history. It is entirely independent of any particular set of laws and institutions. If Ireland was a monarchy or an anarcho-syndicalist commune, it would still be Ireland.

This sense of the permanence and robustness of the nation is especially strong in Irish culture. Its experience is precisely that of the survival of an Irish nation even under the rule and domination of another culture. The whole narrative of Irish nationality is one of indestructibility: it survived everything from invasion and colonisation to famine and mass emigration.

Because of the vagueness of Irish republicanism, there is a strong tendency to confuse the nation and the republic, to imagine that they are the same thing. In this confusion, there is a habit of thinking of the collective entity both as something given and natural and as something durable and indefatigable. It doesn't need to be taken care of because it has shown through the centuries that it can take care of itself. But a republic is completely the reverse. It is not given or natural; it is a collective invention, a choice, a deal that people make with themselves and with each other. And it is not indestructible or indefatigable. It has to be watched over with the vigilance of civic virtue. It has to be recreated again and again. Membership of a nation is accidental and passive; citizenship in a republic has to be conscious and active.

It is perfectly understandable that the newly independent Irish state should be drawn towards the national, rather than the republican, side of this dichotomy. The achievement of national independence, however fraught and problematic, was both a triumph and relief. It might have changed little socially or economically but it provided a deep psychological satisfaction. Something long desired had been attained. It would have been hard to turn the mindset of relief and pride on its head and to say that actually the task of creating a republic had scarcely even begun. And that, even if a republic were built, it would always be in danger of being lost again.

The other, more specific aspect of nationalism that was problematic for republicanism actually came from the opposite direction – a sense not of permanence but of transience. Its focus was on partition and the quest for a United Ireland. This sustained the idea that the Irish state was radically incomplete and therefore temporary. The state was a limbo in which the spirit of the nation had to reside while waiting for admittance to the heaven of a United Ireland. It existed only provisionally, 'pending', in the words of the constitution, 'the reintegration of the national territory'. (It is not accidental that this phrase has overtones of the Catholic imagining of souls waiting for their ultimate appointment with God. It was personally crafted by the Archbishop of Dublin, John Charles McQuaid.[20])

The underlying psychology of this belief was deeply inimical to the task of creating and sustaining a republic. 'The Republic' was by definition something that did not and could not exist within the territory of the state. As with so much else, mainstream southern politics actually hovered continually between this belief and the idea that, for all practical purposes, the existing state was a republic – hence de Valera's inability to say whether or not the state he had created by the 1937 constitution was actually a republic. But in the half of the official brain that still saw the state as a temporary thing, the republic must always be 'pending'. To create a working republic in the south would be like pouring your savings into repairing and beautifying a house rented on a short lease. It could even be seen as a betrayal of the ideal of a United Ireland: if a fulfilled and fulfilling democracy were built in the twenty-six counties, what would happen to the notion that they need the missing six to make them whole?

All of these factors help to explain the weakness of civic virtue for most of the history of the state. What they do not explain, however, is why this culture did not change when the country was apparently transformed in its boom years between 1995 and 2008. Three huge things happened, after all. Ireland became a 'modern' economy of urbanised, industrial or service production. The power of the institutional Catholic Church was broken. And nationalism, in the shape of the quest for a United Ireland, the sense that the southern state was just a temporary contingency, was literally and intellectually disarmed by the peace process and the Belfast Agreement of 1998. If localism, the Church's obsession with sexual morality and the effects of nationalism were major contributors to the weakness of classic republicanism, how come these shifts didn't create the opportunity for it to flourish? Especially since the changes were happening in a context of economic buoyancy, optimism and collective confidence.

Rationally, the effects should have been more favourable to the creation of a republic because one of their most striking manifestations was the breaking of the links between ethnicity, religion and a sense of Irish belonging. On every front, there was a push towards pluralism. The Belfast Agreement enshrined the idea of a plural, complex Irish identity. Internal religious change created much larger faith minorities, both of believers and of non-believers. And the huge influx of migrants from central Europe, Africa and elsewhere added a sudden and profound element of ethnic and cultural diversity. Classical republicanism should have been enormously attractive in this context. On the one hand, it already had a powerful, if contradictory and unfulfilled, existence in Irish culture, so it could not be seen as an alien imposition. On the other, it is the one political ethic that offers a sense of common belonging without appealing to a specific religious or ethnic identity. Yet not only did its time not come, but whatever elements of a republican culture actually existed were in fact further eroded. The republic wasn't remade, it moved steadily towards its present state of complete collapse.

Some of the reasons for this could be seen as accidental, the poor quality of political leadership being the most obvious. But there were deeper reasons, more large-scale forces that operated, not separately, but in association. Each of three positive changes – 'modernity', the breaking of institutional Catholicism and the disarming of mystical nationalism – had, from the point of view of classical republicanism, a dark side.

It is tempting – because largely accurate – to see the failure of Irish public culture to adapt successfully to the opportunities of boom-time prosperity as a result of a resurgence of essentially nineteenth-century habits of mind: an obsession with land and property as the primary source of wealth, the machine politics pioneered by Daniel O'Connell, and a lack of interest in the very technologies that were driving the economy.[21] But international 'modernity', in the form it came in the 1990s, didn't offer an alternative that was especially hospitable to classical republicanism.

Ireland can be said, indeed, to have been unlucky in that it acquired its version of international 'modernity' at a time when the heroic age of that concept was well past. The classic period of the 'modern' state in the West was in the decades between 1945 and 1980. It was not a utopia by any means, but it did have certain key characteristics: a faith in the power of government to create better societies, a consequent prestige for the idea of public service as an admirable ethic, a commitment to the belief that societies should become more equal over time, and an optimistic view of human nature in which altruism, trust, self-sacrifice and mutual benefit were given at least as big a place as the potential for violence, hatred and self-destructive selfishness.

The problem for Ireland was that, just as it was reaching a point where it had its best opportunity to construct a republic, all of these ideas were being systematically dismantled. Beginning with a specific strain in mathematical economics in the United States, the idea took hold that human beings are actually isolated, coldly rational creatures who are programmed to seek only their own advantage. These instincts and desires could best be served and kept in equilibrium by understanding people as both competitors and consumers. They get resources by ruthlessly competing with each other and they express their individuality by using those resources to make consumer choices. Everything else – altruism, 'the public interest', 'public service' – is an illusion. Those who believe in such notions are either idiots or – in this mentality, more admirably – hypocrites, using rhetoric to mask their real pursuit of their own personal advantage.

This notion is literally paranoid: it was formulated in mathematics by John Nash while he was a paranoid schizophrenic who believed that everyone was plotting against him. But it became mainstream economic and political wisdom. Everything of value must be measurable by numbers: hence the ubiquity of numerical 'targets' in all forms of public life. (For example, the time that a home help can spend with an elderly person is now broken down into a series of timed tasks: 10 minutes to get up and dressed, 15 minutes for a shower and so on. Things that cannot be reduced to numbers – holding someone's hand, having a chat – are not measurable and are therefore of no value.) And all public servants, including those in areas such as healthcare and higher education, must be encouraged to think of themselves as competitive individuals pursuing personal interests: hence the ubiquity of 'incentives' to reach 'targets'. The implication of the bonus culture that became the norm is that no one really does anything except for money. The idea that worked well enough for thirty-five years – that people might acquire pleasure, satisfaction and self-worth from doing something that could benefit the community as a whole – was scrapped. That 'modernity' came in this cynical and pessimistic form limited its power to act as a catalyst for a new republican ethic in the boom years.

The changes in the nature of both Irish Catholicism and nationalism also proved to be much less useful to a republican project than they ought to have been. In part, this has to do with the way the changes happened. It would be nice to imagine, in a heroic republican narrative, that they happened on a wave of optimism, when empowered citizens cut off their chains and overthrew oppressive structures of thought. Some of that did happen – aspects of Irish public discourse, especially the rise of movements such as feminism and gay liberation, or in the searing testimonies of survivors of institutional abuse – have had their heady, exhilarating moments. There has been heroic courage. There have been moments when an individual insistence on personal honesty and witness has transformed the way the community has understood itself. If, in the future, a healthy republican democracy wants to erect monuments to its founders and exemplars, it will find plenty of them in the decades after 1960.

But the emotion that destroyed the power of both institutional Catholicism and of warped 'republicanism' was not heroic or triumphal. It was disgust. Violent 'republicanism' ended up disgusting even itself. As its logic became ever more nihilistic in acts such as the Enniskillen and Shankill bombings, it pushed itself to the edge of a moral abyss and realised that it had no choice but to step back. It had to defuse its own intellectual and psychological bombs. The credit it deserved for doing so did not occlude the reality that what was happening was about as heroic as an alcoholic's moment of self-revulsion when the only remaining options are absolute abasement or a reconnection with the everyday world. It didn't help, either, that the act of abstaining from hideous violence was accompanied by the equivalent of the reformed alcoholic's self-satisfaction, the demand to be continually applauded for not being a destructive wreck.

With the institutional Church, disgust had the same centrality. (Again, I emphasise *institutional*. What is at issue is not Catholicism itself but the quasi-monarchical power structure that was built on top of sincere faith.) It is certainly the case that the political power of the Church would have declined gradually in any case. It was ebbing away because of urbanisation, education, the liberation of women, the emergence of new forms of authority through the mass media, the general resistance to obeying diktats in a plugged-in culture. But this process was dramatically short-circuited – by utter disgust. It was the revelation, especially through the extraordinary work of a single journalist, Mary Raftery, of the sheer horror of physical and sexual abuse of children by priests, nuns and religious orders, and the breathtaking cynicism of bishops in covering it up, that transformed the gradual erosion of a system of power into a catastrophic implosion.

Disgust can be a cleansing emotion and in these instances it was both rational and healthy. It was a visceral reaction against two forms of depravity: a nihilistic murder campaign and the enabling – by supposed moral arbiters – of the enslavement and exploitation of the country's most vulnerable children. But if disgust is hygienic, it is also caustic. It is not keyhole surgery; it is radical chemotherapy – it sickens even as it heals. For an Irish person of a Catholic background to look squarely at some of the atrocities committed by 'republicans' in his or her name, or to read the Ryan or Murphy reports on child abuse by religious orders and priests, was to look into the vilest, darkest, most abysmally nightmarish aspects of one's own culture. This was not the Goddess of Liberty storming the barricades of repression. It was the experience of looking into the hideous face of a distinctively Irish and Catholic Medusa and being turned to stone. Objectively, what was happening might have been a liberation, but subjectively it was petrifyingly awful.

Republics are not made up of petrified people. They are created at moments when people feel powerful, when they can sense in every sinew the pulse of civic dignity. Ireland, even in the years of the boom, did not feel like that. It felt betrayed and traumatised. The founding of republics requires a certain concrete illusion, a utopian spirit in which everything seems possible. Republics will settle down into something more sober and qualified, but they need that initial energy of heady hope. This simply wasn't the way Ireland was in those years of glorious opportunity. It was, rather, bombarded with contradictory energies: on the one hand the great buzz of consumerism and a surging, apparently endless property bonanza and on the other the terrible, heart-stopping thud of revelations that everything you believed in – the holiness of clerics, the decency of nationalism, the idea of public service – was a lie. It was much easier to drown out the insistent whisper of the second of these realities with the triumphant roar of the first than to take on the hard task of making a republic.

Being a Republic

How to begin again? By recognising, in the first place, that something is over. The vague, incomplete half-republic that existed between 1922 and 2008 is gone for good. It survives, vestigially, as a puppet show. The institutional forms carry on as if nothing much had happened. Ministers strut around as if they were rulers of a sovereign state – except when they have to explain some especially nasty cutback and plead utter powerlessness, at which point they insist that the troika (the European Central Bank, the International Monetary Fund and the European Commission) made them do it. The Dáil continues to sit in all solemnity as if it did not know that the Bundestag has vastly more power of scrutiny over Irish economic and budgetary affairs than it does. The legal system continues to ponder the constitution, as if it had not been quietly set aside. The citizens even continue to vote in referendums, as if they were a sovereign people whose 'general will' is sacred. Everybody keeps a straight face: deadpan humour is the quintessential Irish mode.

Perhaps this show is necessary to preserve some semblance of collective dignity. There is, after all, a certain kindness in allowing people to save face, to go along with the story of the genteel beggar who tells you he's lost his wallet when you and he know very well that he is merely destitute. Keeping up appearances is not an ignoble or despicable enterprise. Irish culture even has its very own, rather touching phrase for it: 'the relics of old decency': 'When a man goes down in the world, he often preserves some memorials of his former rank, a ring, silver buckles in his shoes &c – the "relics of old decency".'[22]

But we also have to detach ourselves from this theatre of the absurd – to recognise that it is a show, even if, for appearances' sake, we have to carry on with it. This means facing an unpleasant truth: that the relics of old decency is exactly what Irish republicanism currently amounts to. It is the silver buckle in our scuff-heeled, toeless shoes. It still shines with idealism and self-sacrifice and the light of a desire for national dignity. It can bring back powerful memories. But in any form that is real and concrete and current, it is just a reminder of something that we do not now own.

And, in reality, never did. In the run-up to 2016, it is easy to lapse into mourning for the lost republic declared in 1916. But the point, surely, is that it was always lost. Ireland's relationship to its republic is that of a lothario to a conquest – feverish declarations of undying love, a moment of more or less satisfactory coupling and then a long, deep amnesia.

Owning up to this reality does not have to induce cynicism or fatalism – on the contrary. If we had something and lost it, the proper response would be to mourn the death of something precious. There is, on the other hand, a certain sober optimism in facing up to the truth that what we've lost is something that was always vague, half formed, contradictory and ultimately disabling. The Irish republic didn't collapse by accident – it imploded because it was gerry-built. It was philo-sophically incoherent, wide open to corruption and riven by contradictions. It lacked the mortar that holds republics together: the active, conscious consent and commitment of its citizens. The Irish people as a whole never accepted the res-ponsibility of making and minding a republic. But, in their defence, they were never clearly and openly offered that choice.

They do, however, know at least one thing about republics: that there's no point in declaring them. We've done it at least three times and much good it's done us. The gesture may be beautiful (as in 1916) or ridiculous (1949). But a republic is not a gesture. It is a long-term, open-ended contract. It asks hard questions and makes importunate demands: to be awake, to be alive, to be vigilant, to consider one's life as being lived not just in the family home and the immediate locality, not just in the workplace and the shopping mall – valid as all those arenas may be – but in that tough and potentially wonderful place called 'the public realm'.

So, the first task is to be simultaneously hard and easy on ourselves: hard on the illusions about what we have been and what we are now, and easy in the knowledge that realism creates the freedom to begin from scratch. If freedom really is a word for nothing left to lose, the Irish public realm is free. There is nothing to be saved, nothing to be salvaged – and therefore everything to be gained.

The second task is to decide. Lamartine's questions have to be asked and answered: Do you know what you are asking? Do you know what a republic means? Do you think you are prepared to be rulers of yourselves? And perhaps the answer is 'No, thanks.' People such as the present writer wish to imagine that there is no alternative to a radical reinvention of the Irish public realm as a real republic. But this is not true.

There is an alternative to a republic, one that is undoubtedly viable. Irish society and culture, in truth, have a rich bank of experience to draw on: experience of how to survive humiliation, domination, mass unemployment, mass emigration, psychological oppression, abuse and enforced servility. The culture, in many ways, has been shaped precisely by its reaction to these conditions. It adapts brilliantly to circumstances that other societies would find intolerable, not least by deciding that 'it could be worse'. Böll, astutely, noted that this ingrained cultural mechanism isn't merely passive. It is creative, even poetic: 'To persuade someone who has broken his leg, is lying in pain, or hobbling around in a plaster cast that it might have been worse, is not only comforting, it is an occupation requiring poetic talents.' Relativistic fatalism is a superb defence mechanism, drawing on Irish culture's immense resources of imaginative evasion and inventive denial. And, in fairness, this is not an entirely unrealistic impulse. When your history is as grim as Ireland's history is, it is quite logical to look at well-educated emigrants Skyping from Australia and think that it's not as bad as it was when we had an American wake for emigrants because they were effectively dead to their communities in which they were born. It is perfectly reasonable to buckle down to a decade of stumping up extra taxes to pay off the gambling debts of Sean FitzPatrick of Anglo Irish Bank and Michael 'Fingers' Fingleton of Irish Nationwide and think, 'Ah sure, it could be worse. We could be peasants in a thatched cottage having our rent raised because the master gambled us away on the faro table in his London club.'

So there is an option and it is one that is deeply embedded in Irish culture: making the best of a bad job. Arguably no nation on earth is more adept at this task. Irish culture has, quite literally, raised it to a fine art. It is the entire aesthetic of

one of the great Irish geniuses, Samuel Beckett. As Beckett
showed, it is a war we can fight with black humour, a sophisticated sense of irony, even a wistful, lyrical, poetry. The real
Irish national anthem is not 'Amhrán na bhFiann', it is Gloria
Gaynor's 'I Will Survive'. There is, as we also know very well,
a price to be paid for this survival, a psychic distortion that
manifests itself in secret horrors of abuse and depravity. But
there is plenty of sanction from Irish history for the idea that
this is a price worth paying.

There is a decision to be made. Ireland can hunker down
for a long stretch of dependency and domination, and it is
perfectly capable of doing so. Or it can confront the terrify-
ing and exhilarating task of making a republic from scratch.
But before that decision can be made, Lamartine's questions
must be answered: Do you know what you are asking? Do
you know what a republic means? If the first task is to acknowledge and the second to decide, the third is to know.

It is, in these days, rather unfashionable to suggest that
people have a duty to educate themselves. But there's no way
round this embarrassing truth. The basic precondition for a
republic is that the people know what they're doing. That
they should 'know what a republic means'. At the risk of
obnoxious arrogance, it has to be admitted that, in general,
the Irish people do not know what a republic means. This is
not because they are ignorant. It is because 'republican' has
become, in their public culture, a word that deserves either
revulsion or contempt. It calls to mind either the klepto-
cracy of Fianna Fáil The Republican Party or the viciousness
of a self-appointed ethnic militia. Put the word 'republican'
into the search engine of an archive such as that of the *Irish
Times* and 99 per cent of the results will refer either to that
embodied oxymoron, the US Republican Party, currently at

war with every single principle of classical republican democracy, or to some deranged zealot who continues to believe that the only problem with the Irish republic is that not enough people have yet been killed in its name.

This bizarre reality means that Irish people don't just have to learn, they have to unlearn. The very word 'republican' is so debased that there is a very good case for simply abandoning it, at least in the Irish context, to the dustbin of history. What is the point of trying to give meaning to a word that has been so thoroughly corrupted?

The point, in fact, is twofold. There is, as this essay has attempted to sketch, a deep and resonant republican tradition that stretches back over thousands of years and that represents a strain of tolerance, decency and respect for genuine freedom that is remarkably resistant to the pressures of power, cruelty and imperious arrogance. Irish people are, after all, human, and humanity is not so overburdened with sources of hope that it can lightly give up on the few that it has. Republicanism is a form of sober, difficult but genuine optimism in which people make the choice to value the better aspects of their natures.

The second response to the question is itself a question: What is the alternative to this tough hope? Nothing but a surrender to the bleak belief that human beings are isolated, atomised, paranoid machines, programmed by their genes to kick each other in the face. It is society as a system of organised begrudgery. In the short term, such a system is perfectly viable, and the Irish, as a result of their history, are brilliantly adapted to survive within it. But is such a life worth living?

If it is not, then there is a duty to know, to be able to answer the Lamartine question: Do you know what a republic means? There is no avoiding the reality that this involves at least some engagement with the history of an idea. Classical republicanism isn't abstract; it has been formed and forged, tested and tempered, by people trying their best both to imagine and to create a sphere in which, in Philip Pettit's formulation, everyone could hold his or her head high and look everyone else in the eye. But it does demand, especially in the Irish context, the effort of firstly 'unknowing' a tradition of abusive or confused notions of republicanism and secondly engaging with a rich but essentially simple intellectual tradition. That engagement, in turn, has two aspects: the willingness of intellectuals to move out of their comfort zones and set out both to speak and to listen to a much wider public; and the willingness of that public to recognise that the deficit of ideas in Irish public discourse is not rooted in a deep respect for 'popular wisdom'. It is in fact a way of excluding people from power by leaving all important matters to experts, consultants, technocrats and a 'common sense' consensus that is usually a cover for the pursuit of very specific sectional interests.

Is it naive to think that people are willing to make the effort to 'know what a republic means'? Perhaps. But it has happened before. The quarter-century between roughly 1890 and 1916 was a time when hundreds of thousands of Irish people, women and men, engaged themselves in the hard task of trying to understand what a free Ireland would really mean. They went out after long days at work to study hard things: Irish grammar or lace-making or the economics of agricultural co-operation. It is true that they were not, in the end, rewarded with the creation of the republic that their efforts deserved. But they did create that substratum of civic dignity on which a republic could have been built. It is worth something, though, that they deserved better than they got and that the current generation of Irish people has a much softer task. It is already highly literate and sophisticated. The basics of republican philosophy are easy to grasp. But they do come with a condition attached: once grasped, they create civic obligations that are as imposing as they are compelling.

After acknowledgement, decision and knowledge, there is a fourth task: to fight. Republics don't 'come dropping slow,/ Dropping from the veils of the morning to where the cricket sings'. They are born at breaking points. There comes a point at which an existing order becomes intolerable, but that point is itself unpredictable. Who knows precisely which of a billion straws breaks the back of the over-burdened beast that is a citizenry loaded with private debt? The task of republicanism is to identify the right straw.

It is a matter of certainty that Ireland's circumstances of so-called austerity dictated from Berlin and Frankfurt will generate resistance. But, in the absence of a coherent public ethic and a self-respecting citizenry, there is every chance that the breaking point will be one that has no possibility of being a catalyst for something bigger than itself. If the breaking point is septic tanks or a €100 property tax, it will have no purchase on a possible future. It will function merely as a pressure valve, a release of steam after which some meaningless but ostentatious concessions will be made and the general view will be that 'things could be worse'.

Of the many possible final straws, there are, in truth, only two that might spark a real republic in the resulting friction. They are clearly labelled. One is called 'justice' and the other 'equality'. Both, as it happens, are central to the republican project. And this is the fifth task that any ambition to create a republic must face. After acknowledgement, decision, knowing and fighting, come the interlinked struggles for justice and equality. Both are animating principles of the classical republic. And neither, in Ireland's immediate and pressing crisis, have the slightest chance of being addressed in the absence of a real republic. Justice and equality are the forces that make the Irish republic an urgent necessity. Without them, Ireland will be, for the foreseeable future, a Home Rule outpost of a well-meaning but distant Reich. But if they are to mean anything at all, a dignified republic is the only viable possibility.

They sound, of course, like empty pomposities: justice, equality. But concepts cease to be empty and abstract when you experience their precise opposites: flagrant injustice and shameless inequality. And Ireland knows with great clarity what injustice means: the imposition of monumental levels of private gambling debt on the citizenry as a whole. Ireland has been plunged into an existential crisis, not by the stupidities of public policy whose name is legion, but by an utterly incomprehensible and obviously demented decision to assume all private banking debt as a public responsibility. This is a grotesque example of the way injustice results from the absence of a functioning republic. In a republic, the instinctive common sense of citizens would have bridled at the notion that each one of them should work part of his or her day for every day of the foreseeable future to pay off the liabilities of, for example, a German bank that lent money to a private Irish bank that lent it on to an English investor to speculate on an office block in Manhattan.

Basic civic virtue would have prevented this disaster. If the citizenry as a whole had the power it should have in a real republic, the proposition that this same citizenry should be punished collectively for the greed and idiocy of private individuals would not have merited a moment's debate. A republic based on the freedom of its citizens could not possibly allow those citizens to be shackled to obligations they did not, at any point, consent to. Equally, that same citizenry would have a sufficiently strong sense of dignity that it would refuse to accept the injustice of the proposition that an autistic child should be deprived of basic services so that a speculative investor who took a stupid risk on a corrupt bank should have every dollar of his failed gambling stake 'honoured'. A republic would see that its own honour was considerably more at stake in its treatment of a desperately vulnerable child than in its obsequiousness towards a spiv who bought in to a bubble economy at the height of its fantasy. The assumption of a republic is that so-called ordinary citizens understand the idea of justice more clearly than their supposed betters do. The Irish crisis proves the point.

Equality makes the same demand for the necessity of a republic. Even if we accept that so-called 'austerity' is the in-evitable response to the crisis that has overtaken Ireland, any basic idea of public morality would impose one condition: share the pain fairly. But the reality is that a non-republican, Home Rule system will not meet even this minimal standard. In the crudest, most minimal idea of austerity, those who have most would make the largest sacrifices. But Home Rule under Berlin and Frankfurt has had exactly the opposite effect: the poor have borne more of the burden than the rich. Austerity, in its classic meaning in societies such as post-war Britain, cut deeply into the excesses of privilege and narrowed the gap between the top and the bottom. But Ireland's austerity has had precisely the opposite effect. The gap between the lowest earners and highest has actually increased dramatically. In 2009, the top 20 per cent earned 4.3 times what the lowest 20 per cent got. In 2010, the multiple was 5.5 per cent. The over-whelming likelihood is that this trend has been embedded within an 'austerity' project that shows an austere visage towards the weak while smiling warmly on the strong. Which means that, if the project continues for another decade, the result will be a society so divided that it can no longer be imagined as a political community. Ireland will have been repartitioned – this time along the lines not of ethnicity or religion but of class.

Injustice and inequality are now starkly visible. They are the governing principles of the new polity. The choice is either to learn to live with them by forgetting the republic again – this time for good – or to cease to have either to remember or to forget the republic because it has become a reality.

2

The Republic as a Tradition and an Ideal in Ireland Today

ISEULT HONOHAN

Introduction

In Ireland, 'the republic' is an ideal that is readily invoked but its meaning is not entirely clear and unambiguous. There has been a trend in recent times to reclaim it from its identification with the pursuit of national independence through military means, and to use it to represent a broader and more intangible ideal of the kind of society that Ireland could become, with the implication that this has either not yet been fully realised, or that the country has drifted away from it in various ways. Thus recent invocations speak of 'realising', 'reclaiming', or 'renewing' the republic.

The ideal to which we are being recalled is usually seen as specifically Irish, but within a broader European or Atlantic frame. Here I address what republicanism means in the broader tradition, and the way in which Irish republicanism has fitted into this tradition. I suggest that republicanism has something to offer in our current predicament, and conclude by identifying some challenges that arise, and pitfalls that should be avoided.

Republican Ideals

The broad republican tradition originated in Greece and Rome, and was developed in Italian Renaissance city states (especially Florence), seventeenth-century England and in the American and French Revolutions. Republican ideas were articulated in these contexts by thinkers from Cicero through Machiavelli and Rousseau. There have been many different kinds of republics, and republican ideals have been interpreted in many different ways. But we can identify three principal themes that distinguish republicanism from mainstream liberalism, nationalism and other political traditions.

I

It expresses a commitment to realising *freedom in the context of interdependence* among those who are subject to a common power or government.

This is freedom understood in contrast to slavery, or 'non-domination', defined as not being subject to the arbitrary will of others. This is also in contrast to simple 'non-interference' – not being interfered with at any one point in time. The danger of domination arises within society from individuals and groups, as well as from the state. To reduce domination by increasing security from the threat of interference – rather than simply providing recourse to law after the event – is quite demanding. It is achieved firstly through political structures that institutionalise the rule of law; a republic, in James Harrington's term, is 'the empire of *law* and not of men'.[1] The law must give all citizens a significant and secure equal status that allows each to look the other in the eye.[2] In addition, reducing the threat of arbitrary power also requires limiting the concentration of executive power, which can itself be dominating. Thus the rule of law is combined with an emphasis on the dispersal of power – through formal separation of powers, constitutional limits and balances, and measures providing for accountability.

Freedom, on this long-standing and recently rearticulated view, is something that has to be achieved, and it is fragile. It needs more than the legal structures and limits on central-government power that mainstream liberals have tended to emphasise.

2

The second feature of the republican tradition is an emphasis on *self-government*. A republic is a polity of self-governing citizens. It is this, rather than either national independence or the absence of a monarch per se that is implied in the republican idea of the sovereignty of the people. As citizens are interdependent, however, their freedom is not so much a matter of individual autonomy or independence, but of participating in determining, to the extent that this is possible, their joint future. As Hannah Arendt put it, 'the ideal of uncompromising self-sufficiency and mastership is contradictory to the very condition of plurality'.[3] To use the metaphor of authorship that is sometimes invoked in this context, it is not so much a matter of being the sole author of one's life, but being a joint author of the collective life of the polity. It involves the possibility that citizens can be to a greater or lesser extent active in their own self-rule. This may include some degree of representation rather than extensive direct participation, and may be a matter of being enabled and prepared to contest unjust laws and policies rather than continuous involvement in politics; but republicans see politics as a matter of self-government rather than simply representation of interests.

This constitutes one dimension of the 'active citizenship' associated with the republican tradition.

It should be noted that in this tradition, citizens are regarded as people who become interdependent, through a common history, and by virtue of being subject to, and potentially dominated by, the same government – a much broader conception than the nationalist idea of citizenship being defined simply by membership of the same national group.

3

The third feature of republicanism is the idea that a primary goal of politics is *the common good* shared among citizens. The Latin from which the term 'republic' comes, *res publica*, 'the public thing', conveys just this – that the aim of the republic is to provide for the common good, rather than sectional or purely individual interests. This does not mean overriding all individual interests (which would itself constitute domination), but recognising the importance of common interests. Unlike individual interests, common interests are not secured by markets, which even tend to erode them. The rule of law and formal institutions cannot themselves sustain them. This depends also on the attitude of citizens, who internalise the common good, recognise the importance of their common interests, or develop *civic virtue*, which essentially means an inclination to put public shared interests before their private interests where necessary. Because there is a natural tension between individual private and common public interests, this too is a fragile achievement; it does not come naturally. The inherent tendency for individuals to put private interests first is one aspect of corruption. Countering it requires education in awareness of the common nature of common interests, and willingness to consider shared interests and the opinions of others. Hence the importance of education in the republican tradition. (See the discussion in Tom Hickey's essay in this book.) Yet, for republicans personal corruption is part of a wider feature of the fragility of republican self-government, such that institutions tend to decay away from their initial purpose and to need renewal.

This commitment and taking of responsibility constitutes the second dimension of active citizenship.

What Republicanism Is Not

Interpretations of and priorities among these core elements have varied; so have the institutional forms intended to realise them – from unitary to federal, more or less aristocratic to more or less democratic systems. The republic thus cannot be easily identified with any one political form.

The ideal of citizen self-government in the republican tradition is not to be identified simply with 'pure democracy' or majoritarian rule; the aim is not so much to rule others as not to be ruled by them. As Machiavelli wrote, the people in a republic 'neither arrogantly dominate nor humbly serve'.[4]

In addition, although the equal status of citizens implies that there should be certain limits of inequality among citizens, republicanism does not provide a specific economic and social model; it is not socialism. For early modern republicans dependence could be avoided by citizens only if they were property owners; since then, there has been right- and left-wing republicanism, and it has been combined with egalitarian, socialist, conservative, and other positions, some inherently more compatible with it than others. In Marx's work reflecting on the rise of Napoleon III from the revolution in France in 1848, *The Eighteenth Brumaire of Louis*

Napoleon, he dismissed as 'republicans in yellow gloves' the more socially conservative participants among the divided revolutionaries.

What Republicanism Can Offer Today

Even if it does not provide a blueprint for society or support a particular economic strategy, republican ideas have something to offer in this period of crisis and change. They point at least to some important areas we need to reconsider. It should be borne in mind that republican theory in the past has been developed, not by armchair theorists, but by those in the midst of political crisis from Cicero in the dying days of the Roman republic to Machiavelli in Florence threatened by the domination of the Medici, and James Madison in the early United States, attempting to create new institutions to suit a large modern republic.

The ideals of non-domination, participation in self-government, and the dispersal of power are essential to political reform. This requires not just constructing more efficient institutions, but also re-empowering citizens, and finding ways to regulate domination by agents other than the state, whether economic or social.

Such reform, and any politics that might emerge from it, needs to maintain a focus on the common good. But one argument for greater democracy, formalised by the French revolutionary and mathematician Nicolas de Condorcet, and once more now the focus of attention in democratic theory, is that the more people are consulted and the greater the number of different points of view that are brought to bear, the better may be the answers reached to the questions society faces, and that therefore we should not leave these questions to experts. This depends, however, on citizens, in making decisions, being willing to take into account other positions and common interests. Responsible citizenship requires a deliberative approach to political participation. This is the 'jury' model of democracy, as distinct from the 'marketplace' model of democracy, where citizens are thought of as expressing or defending their own interests, and producing a result that represents the best resolution of individual interests.

Finally, economic globalisation and engagement in supranational institutions and international treaties and agreements mean that interdependence (and the threat of domination) extends more intensively beyond state boundaries than ever before. It follows for republican theory that institutional provision for non-domination needs to think beyond national boundaries, and the idea of the republican state, based on interdependence, may be better able to adapt to this than the idea of the national state, based on ethnic affinity or similarity.

Irish Republicanism

In Ireland, republicanism has – at least since the early nineteenth century – been conflated with nationalism, with revolutionary austerity, an authoritarian political style, and especially with separatism from Britain. Thus there has often been a narrow focus on national independence and the means by which it can be secured rather than on freedom and non-domination. (Hence W. B. Yeats's couplet, 'Parnell came down the road and said to the cheering man: "Ireland will get her freedom and you still break stone."')

The range of positions of those who styled themselves republican has led some writers to see it more or less as an inconsistent, empty term.[5] In Ireland, too, as in the broader tradition, it has included positions as divergent as those of James Connolly, Eamon de Valera, Sean O Faoláin and, more recently, Gerry Adams and Michael McDowell. There was a more systematic and coherent tradition of republican thought, articulated most notably by the United Irishmen, that carried right through the nineteenth century.[6] But it has never become the official ideology of the Irish state, as it is in France.

When not confused with nationalism, republicanism has featured in Irish discourse as a call to return to the origins of what is seen as positive in the country. It is especially used to invoke a tradition of non-sectarianism that stretches back to 1798. Indeed, reflecting on the three key ideals of freedom, self-government and the common good, we can see how they can be brought to bear on some of the frequently criticised features of Irish politics: its clientilism represents a form of dependence on representatives rather than on active deliberation by concerned citizens; its centralised government institutions represent the distancing of government from the people; and its traditional localism and more recent tendency towards hedonistic individualism can run counter to the common good. Republicanism in this sense has also been associated in the discourse of both the former President, Mary MacAleese, and her successor, Michael D. Higgins, with the need to focus on the common good and equality of citizens, to move away from individualist consumerism, and for citizens to address political, social and economic issues in terms of constructing their common future as well as amending the practices that brought about the economic and political crisis in the first place.

In this light, more than merely institutional political reform, such as the reduction of the number of TDs, or the abolition of the Senate, needs to be considered. It is not as important that the republic should be mentioned in the constitution, as it is that there should be both greater accountability and a sense of responsibility in the exercise of power. Citizens also need to be able to reclaim some power. This would be more extensive than in the experiment involved in the *We the Citizens* project. (See Elaine Byrne's essay in this book.) But that project at least provided an insight into some of the possibilities and difficulties of a deliberative politics that aims to engage citizens more substantially than current electoral politics in Ireland.

Challenges

Attempting to realise the ideals of the republic in the present very difficult climate involves substantial challenges. These are not all economic. Here I will focus on just two.

First there is the question of how to deal with the increasing diversity of Irish society since the 1990s, and how to integrate immigrants as full members of society or citizens.

From a republican perspective the state is the body of those who are interdependent in their subjection to a common government, and who have developed a common history, rather than some essential pre-political national identity. In so far as immigrants are subject to the power of government, they are at risk of domination. In fact, in contemporary liberal democratic constitutional states immigrants and non-citizens are perhaps those most likely to be subject to the arbitrary and discretionary power of government, whether at their point of entry to the country, in their applications for work or residence status, or in their attempts at family reunification.

They too have a claim to participation in self-government, but they lack full political rights – even though Ireland is more inclusive than many other countries in granting local voting and standing rights to all residents. While the general requirements for acquiring citizenship through naturalisation are not particularly onerous compared with other European countries, the fact that the process is still ultimately subject to ministerial discretion needs to be addressed.

There is also the question of how much accommodation should be made to both indigenous and immigrant cultural and religious practices. Here again, we should think twice before assuming that the French model of the republic, which is strictly neutralist and secularist (in, for example, banning women from covering their faces in public), is the only or necessarily best way to go. Rather than a neutralist (or hands-off) approach to cultural and religious diversity, which allows people to carry on cultural and religious practices in private but insists on a neutral public realm, an even-handed approach may be more compatible with the republican principle of non-domination. Such an approach would acknowledge the particularity of citizens, and aim to accommodate different practices to which they are committed, where there are no serious reasons based in justice that do not outweigh them.[7] The increasing diversity of Irish society requires us also to rethink what it means to be Irish. This is a process that has hardly begun, though the extensive reflection on Irish identity over the last forty years and the attempt to create a more generous definition that could include the Protestant and Unionist population in Northern Ireland, offers an encouraging precedent.

The second challenge is what it means to be a republic in a world of global interdependence. It is no longer (if it ever was) appropriate to conceive of the world as a set of wholly autonomous or self-sufficient states, each sovereign in at least four dimensions – internally with respect to their populations, externally with respect to other states and also to individuals seeking admission to the territory and to membership in the state, and internationally as having the capacity to engage in international agreements. The fact of international inter-dependence and the potential for domination across borders requires a rethinking of republican theory itself – and a more nuanced account of sovereignty, in terms not of the state but of the people, and in terms not of mastery, but of non-domination. In such an approach, sovereignty would not imply complete independence of international political institutions, but rather security from arbitrary external interference through, for example, greater accountability of international institutions, and more democratic engagement in their decision-making.[8] This, as we have seen, is a challenge for republican theory itself, but one it might have the resources to meet.

Pitfalls to Be Avoided

There are a number of pitfalls that can arise in connection with the invocation of republican ideas. These are not necessarily inherent in republicanism, though they may result from its misinterpretation. I shall mention four.

The first pitfall, which is associated with popular sovereignty, is *populism*. This represents the body of citizens, 'the people', as an abstract, homogeneous entity. Perhaps it would help to understand the ideal of popular sovereignty as entailing that 'people' are self-ruling, rather than that there is something called 'the' people, which is self-ruling. There is a truth that underlies populism: that it is people and not the state or its appointed or elected officials that are sovereign, and that contemporary liberal democratic government has distanced itself from its citizens and tended to monopolise power. But populist approaches, in reaction to this, tend to draw an exaggerated contrast between the people and an internal or external enemy, whether this be identified as elites, political parties, corrupt politicians, strident minorities, or the media and others.[9] They may offer simplistic solutions, which reject the complex procedures and compromises that politics entails. Furthermore, those who call on the authority of the people may be self-appointed spokesmen, closer to AstroTurf than grass roots. If such movements are authoritarian and exclusionary in their definition of the people, and oppose all established institutional power, they may undermine the possibility of citizens actually becoming empowered and involved in decisions about their future.

While excessive individualism or self-interest, and the way that this fed into unthinking support for many neoliberal positions, may have been the besetting vice of the Celtic Tiger period, it may be that populism is a comparable danger now.

A second pitfall, associated with active citizenship, is an *overemphasis on service* or the responsibility of citizens at the expense of empowering them. This focus on service is a widespread tendency, which can be seen in the direction taken by the Taskforce on Citizenship, set up by Bertie Ahern when Taoiseach, and in the 'Big Society' programme of David Cameron's government, and has long been a tendency in formal citizenship education. Where responsibility and commitment is expected, divorced from extending the resources or capacity of people to act, and independent of participation in political decision-making, citizens can end up being subject to increased domination.

Thirdly, as already noted, it is a mistake to take other models, for example the USA or France, as a blueprint or essential realisation of a republic. This is quite common among com-

mentators in Ireland. France is indeed the state most self-conscious of its republicanism, but it is a very specific realisation, developed in the context of France's unique history.
Moreover, in facing the challenges of dealing with diversity
and globalisation, it has not necessarily adopted the laws and
policies most appropriate for a republicanism that wishes to
deal justly with cultural diversity.[10] In any case, to determine
what kind of republic is possible in Ireland, it is necessary to
examine what follows from basic republican principles, given
our particular history and where we find ourselves now.

Finally, in response to the pressures and constraints from
Europe and beyond that have been a result of the economic
crisis, there is a risk of invoking republicanism to support a
form of isolationism. While it is beyond question that our loss
of sovereignty needs to be addressed, there is also a need to
work out what sovereignty might mean in an interdependent
world – and whatever this will be, it will not be self-sufficiency or withdrawal from international institutions. 'Sinn
féin', the historic slogan, might be better translated as 'we
ourselves'– taking initiatives and assuming responsibility –
rather than 'ourselves alone' – cutting off connections – as it
has often been understood in the past.

Republicanism cannot simply be taken ready-made off the
rack. For those who see the republic as an ideal yet to be
realised, there is a task ahead in reimagining it as a polity
that protects its citizens from domination from other agents
and groups in society and from state power, both within the
state and externally. And there is a job to be done in thinking
about what institutions best promote non-domination and the
common good, and what it means for both indigenous
residents and newcomers to be a citizen of a republic.

3

The Democracy of a Republic

ELAINE BYRNE

Democracy means rule by the people for the people but that does not mean that democracy is actually democratic. Democratic reform in the ninetieth and twentieth centuries meant the extension of the franchise irrespective of gender, property rights and age. The democratic reformers of the twenty-first century are less concerned about the quantity of opportunities to participate – that battle has largely been won – but rather on the quality of that participation. The focus instead will be on the capacity to impact meaningfully on decision-making rather than the paltry endorsement of a fait-accompli policy agenda.

The principles of liberty, equality and autonomy are not always best served through the collective expression of voting. If they were, parliaments around the world would not be dominated by well-educated, middle-class, middle-aged men but would reflect the age, gender, ethnicity and socio-economic background of the society they seek to represent. Democracy is, by its very nature, flawed. Majority rule often disappoints because it produces decisions that are determined by what is popular, as opposed to what is 'best'. The popular good and the public good compete with one another in a system that rewards short-term decision-making while encouraging the illusion of immediate and positive outcomes for the majority.

Participation is ultimately determined by individual self-interest disguised as collective action.

The global economic crisis exposed the fundamental weakness of this limited conception of democracy. The genesis of Ireland's current structural deficit was conceived by the 2002 and 2007 election contests. This was a period defined by auction politics for the purpose of achieving power. The manifestos of political parties were contradictory: they simultaneously promised low taxes and high public spending. The faculty for informed long-term decision-making is limited when there is an absence of knowledge and independent sources of truth. Democracy does not guarantee that the best decisions are made because the public have an insatiable demand for uncomplicated expediency.

This is the very antithesis of a republic. Well, at least the notion of what we in Ireland consider a republic to be. The violent struggle to fulfil the audacious demands of the 1916 proclamation of independence cost almost five thousand lives in the War of Independence and the Civil War. A further 3,722 died during the thirty-year conflict in Northern Ireland known colloquially as 'The Troubles'.

This human sacrifice for an Irish republic has been offered again and again in the absence of any proper definition or acknowledgement of what a republic is. Here lies Ireland's deepest contradiction. The Irish constitution does not contain the word republic. Although the 96 words of John A. Costello's 1948 Republic of Ireland Act state that Ireland is officially a republic, it never goes beyond this legal statement. Thousands may have died for the principle of republicanism but they did so without any formal expression of it since the 1916 proclamation.

If anything, the notion of a republic is an abstract political philosophy that was inherited by accident. Ireland's greatest revolutionaries were ambiguous about their ambitions for a republic. 'The British form of government was monarchical. In order to express clearly our desire to depart from all British forms, we declared a Republic.' Michael Collins went on to explain in his only published work, the *Path to Freedom*, that Ireland 'repudiated the British form of government, not because it was monarchical but because it was British. We would have repudiated the claim of a British Republic to rule over us as definitely as we repudiated the claim of the British monarchy.'

So, what can be done? What is the optimal means of ensuring that individual citizens decide what the 'best' possible collective decision should be? How can this be achieved within the context of a republic? Is it possible to marry the different ideals of democracy and republicanism? This essay seeks to explore how the quality of participation in the Irish polity can be improved. In doing so, it considers the contemporary challenges to democratic action.

Trilateral Commission 1975: Too Much Democracy

An influential book published in 1975, *The Crisis of Democracy: Report on the Governability of Democracies to the Trilateral Commission*, argued that the revolutionary decade of the 1960s had produced an 'excess of democracy'. Founded by David Rockefeller in 1973, the Trilateral Commission sought to 'bring together experienced leaders within the private sector to discuss issues of global concern', particularly between Europe, the United States and Japan. Only 'apathy and non-involvement' by citizens would ensure that order could be maintained. The expectations of citizens had to be lessened. Demands for greater democratic participation were dismissed. The political roadmap advocated by the Trilateral Commission, called for a pronounced reduction in the role of government through deregulation and privatisation and a confined public space. A crisis of democracy existed because there was simply too much democracy.

The Trilateral Commission demanded duty-based conformism, where participation in the bargaining process of democracy was narrowly confined to those who vote in each electoral cycle. Concepts of citizenship have traditionally stressed the responsibilities of citizenship and reinforced the existing political order and authority patterns. This elitist, top-down, model of democracy envisages a limited role for the citizen. This was especially evident in the intellectual assumptions underlying neoliberal thought in the 1970s, and so strikingly expressed in the Trilateral Commision's report.

People now, after three decades of unregulated free-market economics, wish to engage more in democracy, rather than merely voting for a political party once every few years. The definition of political participation has expanded into new forms of action such as signing petitions, joining citizen interest groups and engaging in unconventional forms of political action. Many people prefer to join public interest groups, social movements and NGOs rather than political parties. Political action is now characterised by direct forms of communication through the internet and mobile phones, by the emergence of generalised anti-establishment sentiment, the demand for democratic innovation and for the devolution of decision-making. This sea-change in citizens' expectations has occurred because attitudes to authority have simultaneously undergone a radical transformation.

This was especially evident in Richard Stengel's explanation for making Facebook's Mark Zuckerberg *Time Magazine*'s

2010 Person of the Year. 'There is an erosion of trust in authority, a decentralizing of power and at the same time, perhaps, a greater faith in one another.' The managing editor of *Time* also noted that Facebook 'has wired together a twelfth of humanity into a single network thereby creating a social entity almost twice as large as the US'. The boundaries of public and private, of openness and secrecy, will never be the same again.

Internet-based organisations such as Anonymous and WikiLeaks share Facebook's ethos of self-actualisation and autonomy but have taken it one step further by directly confronting influential gatekeepers who control the political and communications agenda. Anonymous, a decentralised online community, acts in a co-ordinated manner to attack the technological abilities of organisations through what is known as a distributed denial of service (DDoS). Such acts of civil disobedience have included attacks on the government websites of Tunisia, Egypt, Iran, Australia, Brazil, France, the United States and Ireland. Julian Assange's WikiLeaks imposed transparency on the world's only remaining super power with the release of 251,287 diplomatic cables that have proved embarrassing to the United States.

Anonymous and WikiLeaks have sought to defy the modus operandi of highly secretive elite institutions and redistribute information back into the hands of citizens. These republican-minded actions are the very antithesis of the traditional notions of authority espoused by the Trilateral Commission, which emphasised the values of obedience, unwavering loyalty and deference to centralised hierarchical structures.

The same is true of the global protest movements of the Arab spring, the Indignants movement in Spain and the global Occupy movement, which are woven together with the same underlying motivation to challenge unaccountable centres of economic and political power. Disproportionately well educated and young, these citizen-led initiatives are formed without encouragement from or endorsement by existing political forces. 'The power of the people is greater than the people in power' became the Egyptian pro-democracy slogan. All of these movements share in the belief that their countries' political systems and economies are dysfunctional and corrupt. All demand more accountable democratic structures with more meaningful prospects for people to participate in their own destinies. No surprise then that *Time* described 'The Protester' as 'fervent small-d democrats' in their conferral of the 2011 Person of the Year.

At the outset, it appeared that by virtue of their critical mass – rule by the people – the internet phenomena of Facebook, Anonymous, WikiLeaks and the global protest groups were redefining the social contract. The extent to which they changed the rules of the game remains to be seen. By mid-2012, the Occupy movement had dissipated, Islamism and military power had strangled the Arab spring and Assange's credibility was undermined by allegations of sexual crimes. None the less, by virtue of their existence and their underlying demands for greater democratic freedoms, these phenomena have punctured previous narratives of how participation was defined.

Deliberative Democracy

The existing challenges to democracy offer the possibility for the democratisation of democracy – the fulfilment, in a way, of the aspirations of the 1960s generation, which were denied by the Trilateral-style mindsets of the 1970s and 1980s governments, symbolised by the authoritarian populism of Thatcher and Reagan.

There is a crisis of trust in Irish public life. In the 2009 Eurobarometer poll, Ireland recorded virtually the lowest level of public trust in its political institutions across the twenty-seven European countries surveyed, with only Hungary, Latvia, Lithuania and Greece registering lower degrees of trust. This is not unique to Ireland. The Organisation for Economic Co-operation and Development (OECD) also observed in the same year, 'The financial crisis revealed failures of governance.' The OECD warned, 'For the sake of keeping the trust of voters, governments also need to be able to reassure citizens that their affairs are in safe hands.'

There is no magic-bullet solution to restore this trust. Governments and civil society in Iceland, Brazil, Canada and elsewhere have increasingly resorted to deliberative democracy as a mechanism to improve the process of decision-making. The fall in confidence and the perceived weakening of participation in formal politics has corresponded with the perception that a democratic deficit exists. Does this collapse in trust therefore demand a departure from the traditional institutional architecture of politics?

This renewal can be accomplished through deliberative democracy. This process emphasises the broad participation of citizens in the operation of political systems. It is an alternative means of reaching collectively binding decisions through reasoned agreement. Citizens have the opportunity to express their views and preferences and justify their decisions within this auxiliary institution, which serves to complement existing parliamentary structures. Above all, it improves the quality of participation. The renewed expectations of civil society, in terms of enhanced good governance and citizen empowerment, can deepen democracy by introducing 'lay' perspectives into policy areas where there has been limited involvement of citizens in decisions that profoundly affect their lives.

The pooling of knowledge and the sharing of life experiences widens the breadth of public understanding on complex issues. It can serve to educate the wider population. Deliberative democracy also has the potential to inject popular legitimacy into any proposed reform because it introduces transparency and accountability into policy-making by encouraging citizens to scrutinise the decisions of their representatives. Moreover, it promotes greater popular engagement with democratic institutions because it gives citizens the power to take ownership of decisions.

Political decisions are ultimately about making trade-offs between competing interests. The scarcity of goods in a democracy forces elected representatives to determine how best to distribute limited resources. The decisions about and delivery of these goods have tended to operate within a closed and secretive system. Irish politics, for instance, has in the past been captured by vested interests. The 'bricks and beef' cabals of developers and cattle barons have unduly influenced the formulation of public policies, laws and regulations for their private benefit.

Open scrutiny of the criteria and justifications used for the allocation of public commodities therefore helps to expose inequalities within the system. It also gives expression to the very definition of a republic where the supreme power rests in the body of citizens and not the vested interests of a few. The 'best' possible collective decision can be made only when the citizen body actively contributes to choices made on its behalf.

The definition of a republic also entails that the supreme power that rests within the citizen body is ultimately exercised by representatives chosen directly or indirectly by them. The necessity to engage in trade-offs, and the difficult decisions that this demands, is often not fully appreciated by a public that has to bear the costs of such decisions. The capacity of politicians to justify their decisions to the public is quite low in a climate that is distinguished by a fervent distrust of politics. Anti-politics has to be replaced by more realistic democratic mechanisms.

Deliberative Democracy in Ireland: *We the Citizens*

Deliberative democracy was tested throughout Ireland in 2011 in a civil-society initiative, generously funded by Atlantic Philanthropies. Elaine Byrne, David Farrell, Eoin O'Malley and Jane Suiter were members of the academic team.

We the Citizens had two distinct stages, at regional and national level. Seven open-door, open-agenda events were organised in Blanchardstown, Tallaght, Letterkenny, Athlone, Kilkenny, Cork and Galway. The regional events partially informed the agenda of a subsequent national Citizens' Assembly in Dublin. The formula was simple. The process of deliberation was the same for both the regional and national events. Members of the public participated in a round-table facilitated meeting, which encouraged a constructive rather than negative dialogue. Each table had a facilitator who fostered discussion by ensuring that everyone had the opportunity to speak and that no single person dominated the conversation. The deliberative format was designed to give everyone the opportunity to raise their own viewpoints and to allow for disagreement. This consensus-building technique – through argument and justification – facilitated greater engagement and mutual respect. The tone of the debates was noticeably non-aggressive and allowed for issues to be discussed freely and openly. The participants at both the regional and national events welcomed the depoliticised nature of the deliberation. 'Eoin', for instance, contrasted this experience with the confrontational and adversarial tenor of parliamentary debates: 'The Dáil is all about verbally defeating your opponent's argument. People don't really listen to one another. If someone has a 180-degree u-turn on something, it's regarded as a sign of weakness rather than a response to logic.'

A series of polls was carried out by in a professional polling company before the national Citizens' Assembly met. Ipsos MRBI asked a representative sample of the Irish population a number of survey questions. Some of these questions were framed as a consequence of the issues that emerged from the regional events. Ipsos MRBI recruited 100 people from this original sample of 1,242 people to attend the Citizens' Assembly. In the weeks following the Assembly, Ipsos MRBI carried out a second series of surveys, to see if participants' opinions had shifted because of their involvement in the deliberative experiment and to what extent.

Participants represented a cross-section of Irish society in terms of age, gender, ethnicity, religion and socio-economic background. In other words, they were a better mirror image of the Irish population than those elected to the parliamentary legislature. As 'Áine' said, 'The people here looked like me. When I watch Oireachtas reports, the politicians are usually male, middle-class teachers, farmers and barristers.'

The Evidence

The polls showed statistically significant changes as a consequence of participation in the deliberative experiment. Not only did people's opinions shift on policy issues, but citizens felt more empowered because of their involvement in the Citizens' Assembly. This is borne out in the evidence presented in Table 1. On a scale of 1 to 7, where 1 is strongly disagree and 7 is strongly agree, participants had a greater interest in politics, a greater willingness to discuss politics and a decline in the belief that ordinary people have no influence.

Table 1

	Interest in Politics	Willingness to discuss politics	More willing to get involved in politics	Ordinary people have no influence?
Before Citizens' Assembly	5.22	5.2	4.51	4.42
After Citizens' Assembly	5.7	5.65	5.74	4.0

The biggest change observed was a willingness to become more involved in politics. The *We the Citizens* experiment conferred a belief among participants that they had the ability to influence outcomes. This was very noticeable over the course of the weekend. People developed confidence as the two days progressed. This was especially evident among women and young men. Participants said that they had never taken part in lengthy political discussions because they did not think their opinions mattered. When they were given the chance to voice their views, they did so with growing self-assurance.

This was particularly pronounced among women. Before the process, 35 per cent of female participants believed that they could have no influence on politics, and this feeling of impotence diminished by 14 points to 21 per cent after the process. This suggests that the deliberative method not only encourages a greater parity of participation but supports the evidence that women are turned off by the adversarial nature of formal politics. A sentiment shared by a female participant, 'Roisin': 'What I got out of this was that it took the discussion on politics away from the politicians. I got to participate about the questions that affect my daily life. For one evening at least, that made a change.'

Aside from the evidence demonstrating increased trust in political action, *We the Citizens* also proved that participants' opinions shifted on policy issues when they had the opportunity to become better informed and to debate the trade-offs associated with them.

Expert witnesses provided testimony on a range of topics such as economic issues and political reform. To that end, the Citizens' Assembly members heard from two fiscal specialists who represented very different sides of the argument on tax increases and spending cuts. Fergal O'Brien of the Irish Business and Employers Confederation (IBEC), told the participants that 'it would be impossible to achieve a balanced budget without reducing public expenditure'. He acknowledged that 'some tax increases' might be necessary though the Irish industry spokesperson believed that 'the bulk of the adjustment must be on the expenditure side'. In contrast, Dr Nat O'Connor of the left-leaning TASC (Think Tank for Action on Social Change), outlined why he was 'generally opposed to cuts' and instead advocated for 'increased taxation to pay for quality public services'.

This access to balanced information facilitated reflective judgements by participants and the time to develop preferences.

'John' stated the obvious about his experiences in the Assembly: 'When we shared the information among ourselves it turned out that what we were actually doing was pooling our knowledge and our life experiences. It was like being on a jury.'

The survey results found that there were considerable effects on the attitudes of the participants when it came to economic beliefs. The fiscal position of the attendees at the *We the Citizens* initiative moved significantly on every economic question they were asked. As Table 2 shows, 48 per cent of participants were in favour of the sale of state assets before the Citizens' Assembly met but this had fallen to 10 per cent when the same individuals were polled after the event. As a consequence of increased information and the space they were given for deliberation, over a third of participants reversed their views on the sale of state assets. On the question of property tax, just 40 per cent of participants were in favour before the weekend, but this jumped to 56 per cent by the end of the weekend. A similar shift took place on the question of water charges with a 25 per cent change in attitudes before and after, adjusting from 60 per cent in favour to 85 per cent.

Table 2

	In favour of property tax	In favour of water charges	In favour of the sale of state assets
Before the Citizens' Assembly	40%	60%	48%
After the Citizens' Assembly	56%	85%	10%

Lessons from Ireland

The Citizens' Assembly model offers three possible alternatives for democratic engagement:

1 The Citizens' Assembly produces a specific proposal for change that may be directly acted upon by the government in the form of a legislative act.

2 In a case where a matter has constitutional significance, the Citizens' Assembly produces the wording for the referendum question. This may go to a parliamentary committee for consideration or be put to the people in a referendum.

3 In the case where the matter in question relates to local budgetary issues, the decision of the Citizens' Assembly should have a direct impact on a portion of budgetary expenditure in the local area.

The evidence proves that participants are more disposed to accept tax increases as a consequence of expert testimony and deliberation. However the methodological framework in which this data was collected must also be considered. The time allocated for the IBEC and TASC evidence was fifteen minutes, or seven and half minutes each. The time spent on deliberation of the three policy areas, relating to property taxes, water charges and the sale of state assets, was one hour in total or twenty minutes each. These debates were fractured and the feedback by participants noted that they had insufficient time for discussion.

None the less, a shift in opinions did occur. 'Aoife', for example, was adamant about her opinions before her participation: 'I wasn't sure what the point of me coming to the Citizens' Assembly was. I have very fixed opinions on lots of things. My mind was made up a long time ago on a range of issues.' Aoife was 'surprised because my opinion changed on some things when I got new information from the expert witnesses who made me think differently about some of the topics'. Changes of mind were also observed on the questions of political reform that were discussed. For instance, deliberation on the role of Dáil deputies prompted participants to assert that TDs should concentrate more on national legislative and policy work and less on local services.

The reason why people's views and attitudes changed varied. The facilitators who moderated the deliberations were aware the extent to which the tone and ethos of the debate ensured that participants genuinely listened to one another. This was evident in the case of two participants who had distinctly diverse life experiences. 'John' was very pro-environment while 'Shauna' was very pro-business and entrepreneurial and rarely gave much thought to the environment. However, after hearing the thoughts of John, Shauna said she had never considered how the environment can be part of economic growth rather than the two being mutually exclusive. Michael Courtney, the facilitator of that discussion, believed that Shauna's 'way of thinking had been significantly affected by someone who she would otherwise never have met'.

Public debate often becomes polarised into black or white positions. 'Playing the man, not the ball' becomes the de facto approach for an anti-intellectual public discourse that feeds on straw men. The space for pluralist discussion narrows when the opportunity to engage with those from different socio-economic, generational, ethnic, gender or even professional backgrounds is limited. The randomness of the selection was crucial. This cross-cutting participation exposed individuals to dissimilar views from that of their normal life experience. A willingness to accept unfamiliar points of view of course depends on how open people are to alternative stances.

We the Citizens prioritised deliberation on political reform issues such as gender quotas, the role of TDs, reform of the Seanad (the upper house of the Irish parliament) and the electoral system rather than matters relating to Ireland's relationship with the European Union, membership of the euro, the possibility of default on the national debt, the deficit and the conditions imposed on the Irish population by the EU–IMF–ECB bailout. Although they were a feature of the discussions at the regional events, the original Ipsos MRBI survey did not focus on these questions. These issues were regarded as too contentious and politically unsound for the Assembly process, a view not shared by this author, who served as a member of the academic team on the project.

If the objective of a Citizens' Assembly is to include citizens more directly in decision-making, then the agenda of any such deliberation is best informed by the issues that citizens themselves wish to discuss. The public legitimacy of a truly deliberative process is dependent on the avoidance of what political theorists call 'salience transfer'. According to agenda-setting theory, salience transfer refers to the ability of particular stakeholders to transfer their agendas or issues onto the public agenda. It is only when citizens feel that they own the agenda from the outset that the process itself can capture public imagination. The Fine Gael–Labour government established the Irish Constitutional Convention in 2012. There was no consultation with the public regarding the topics for discussion. A third of the Convention's seats were reserved for political representatives which defeats the very notion of deliberative democracy.

A depoliticised process may be politically expedient because it deprioritises certain issues. As 'Eadaoin' observed during the Citizens' Assembly weekend, 'I'm concerned that if a Citizens' Assembly is introduced by the government for some decisions, it will be used by politicians to give the perception of legitimacy but will actually diffuse momentum for change.' A clear policy implementation process is therefore necessary to ensure that decisions are followed through with political action.

Is it realistic though for deliberative democracy to act as a fourth popular branch of government? Can decisions made through this process claim greater legitimacy than those in a representative democracy? The establishment of a fourth branch of government is not without its difficulties. It would necessitate a clear relationship and power structure in its relations with the judiciary, the executive and the legislature. An institutionalised system of checks and balances is necessary. A fourth branch would necessitate the redefining of roles. If the legislature represents the representative branch of democracy, the executive is popularly elected and the judiciary is appointed, which branch of government would have the legitimacy to curb this new fourth branch?

The Corruption of Democracy

Deliberative democracy offers the possibility of embracing republican ideals at a time when the democratic deficit has widened very sharply. The lack of trust in Irish institutions, as identified earlier, can only have multiplied with the deepening of the global economic crisis. The public's expectations about its democracy have been undermined. Irish citizens are no longer remote from decision-making; they are completely removed from it because the representative function of democracy has been made redundant.

The intervention of the IMF, the ECB and the EU into Irish domestic policy-making has warranted the introduction of conditionality into every aspect of internal decision-making. The IMF defines conditionality as an agreement by a government to 'adjust its economic policies to overcome the problems that led it to seek financial aid from the international community'. This reliance on international organisations is diluting democracy. Rule by the people for the people is emasculated when the policy straitjacket of conditionality is worn. When governments sign up to loan agreements, their decision-making capacity is limited because of the conditional nature of such arrangements. This loss of economic sovereignty was nowhere more apparent than the German Bundestag's review of confidential details of the Irish budget in November 2011, three weeks before the Irish parliament debated the measures and again in March 2012. The Tánaiste (deputy prime minister) Eamon Gilmore said he was 'unhappy' about these incidents.

The real effect of external participation in a country's domestic affairs is ultimately the decline of democratic practices. The forces that drive IMF policies – heavily influenced by the major Western powers – have in the past been accused of being insensitive to their social impact. When the burden of structural readjustment falls disproportionately on those who depend on social and public services, the upshot is civil unrest. As happened in Greece in 2011, the government feels that it has no other option but to limit civil liberties in the attempt to subdue the social upheaval that results from the stark structural readjustment prescribed by the IMF and others. The deep sense of public contempt for the political class can then potentially cannibalise the very belief in the possibility of political action. The overwhelming perception that a country's institutions are weak, incompetent and illegitimate feeds into the destructive notion that politics is futile.

This belief in the ineffectual nature of politics gained support among some unlikely bedfellows on the left and the right in Ireland. Both argued that non-elected parliamentarians should become ministers. Fianna Fáil's 2011 pre-election manifesto contained many of the same reform proposals that appeared in a document circulated to leading public figures by one of Ireland's wealthiest and most controversial businessmen, Dermot Desmond. Peter Sutherland, chair of Goldman Sachs International and European honorary chair of the Trilateral Commission, assisted with the document.

Authored by two Irish political scientists, *Ireland First: Political Reform – Effective and Efficient Government* called for the appointment of external Ministers. It did however include the polite concession to democracy that 'in order to maintain the link with voters . . . a majority of the cabinet should have been elected as TDs'. Democratic legitimacy is now considered an unnecessary extravagance or an optional extra. The indignity of asking the public for their trust through the democratic apparatus of voting is routinely dismissed and steadily eroded.

The response to economic crisis throughout Europe has been to reject the principle of democracy: rule by the people, for the people. The instinct of power is to preserve and amplify itself. The Irish government's 'radical' political reform agenda is defined by initiatives, such as abolishing the Seanad, that seek to reinforce a centralisation of power through the camouflage of popular support. This trend is very pronounced within the newer democracies of Eastern Europe. Prime Minister Viktor Orban, for example, deliberately undermined the independence of key parts of the Hungarian state in December 2011. His constitutional reforms included the removal of traditional democratic checks and balances on the government such as the autonomy of the central bank and the judiciary.

Trilateral Commission 2009 and Too Much Democracy (Again)

In a 2009 keynote speech, entitled 'The Intellectual Underpinnings of the Trilateral Partnership in the 21st Century', Henry Kissinger sought to redefine the role of the Trilateral Commission. In 1975, it was the 'excess of democracy' that was perceived as the cause of political stability. Now, 'the fundamental flaw of the globalized economic system . . . was that the economic model and the political model' are, Kissinger believes, 'out of sync with each other'. Noting that the 'political world is in a period of fundamental change' and that 'governments are so preoccupied with immediate issues', the Trilateral Commission, he contended, could 'indicate direction' on how sovereignty is defined in the multipolar international system.

Enter the technocratic, unelected leaders of Greece and Italy, Lucas Papademos and Mario Monti, who became prime ministers in 2011. Papademos is a former vice president of the European Central Bank, governor of the IMF for Greece and member of the Trilateral Commission. Monti is a former European Commissioner, adviser to Goldman Sachs and European chairman of the Trilateral Commission. The Italian was sworn in as a senator for life in November 2011 and appointed as both Prime Minister and Minister of Economy and Finance a week later. Papademos and Monti were tasked with the implementation of harsh austerity budgets in their domestic economies, measures conceived by the international organisations that had previously employed both of them. The Fine Gael–Labour 2011 programme for government proudly proclaimed that with 'the stroke of a pen, in thousands of polling stations' a 'democratic revolution' had taken place. The coalition had secured the largest parliamentary majority in the history of the state 'with an absolute resolve to bring the change the people so clearly demand'. Yet the ECB and the IMF maintained that Ireland's economic programme had been negotiated on behalf of the state rather than on behalf of a particular government. Olli Rehn, EU Economic Commissioner, wryly remarked, 'The EU has signed the Memorandum of Understanding with the State, with the Republic of Ireland, and we expect continuity and respect of the memorandum.' He made these comments just a week before the general election and tellingly said, 'If there will be any changes . . . it will take place for the overall European reasons not specifically because of electoral statements in Ireland.'

Voters can change governments but they cannot change the policies of international organisations, bondholders and external lenders. Ireland's 'democratic revolution' has been replaced by unaccountable technocracy, just as it has in Italy and other established democracies. Antonis Samaras's election as the Greek Prime Minister in June 2012 merely represented a continuation of Papademos's measures. Like Papademos, Samaras has vowed to reduce Greece's total debt to 120 per cent of GDP by 2020 under the terms of its international loan agreement with the troika.

Since the economic crisis began in 2008, some €25 billion, almost 15 per cent of current gross domestic product, has been removed from the Irish economy. Yet the terms of the IMF–ECB–EU troika programme dictate that Ireland is only halfway through its recovery plan.

It was Marcus Tullius Cicero who introduced the teachings of Greek philosophy to his native Rome. He railed against those in power who had corrupted political action through power struggles and dictatorship. 'A nation can survive its fools, and even the ambitious,' Cicero wrote in 45 BC.

But it cannot survive treason from within. An enemy at the gates is less formidable, for he is known and carries his banner openly. But the traitor moves amongst those within the gate freely, his sly whispers rustling through all the alleys, heard in the very halls of government itself.

For the traitor appears not a traitor; he speaks in accents familiar to his victims, and he wears their face and their arguments, he appeals to the baseness that lies deep in the hearts of all men. He rots the soul of a nation, he works secretly and unknown in the night to undermine the pillars of the city, he infects the body politic so that it can no longer resist.

For Cicero, the republic was *res publica*, the Latin term that translates as 'public affairs'. The republic is the foundation of order and political stability because of its emphasis on civic virtue. Only the knowledgeable citizen can become the competent citizen.

Deliberative democracy is one means by which the quality of participation in a democracy can be enhanced. That assumes we still have a democracy in the first place.

4
Civic Virtue, Autonomy and Religious Schools: What Would Machiavelli Do?

TOM HICKEY

A republic, fundamentally, is a political community that protects the liberty of its citizens. Republicans have a distinct understanding of liberty: to enjoy liberty is to enjoy equal protection from 'domination', where domination is defined as arbitrary or unchecked power.[1] If I enjoy that status, I can be confident that no individual or group of individuals, whether in the public or in the private sphere, has the capacity to interfere at will in my choices. There will be interference in my choices, of course. That much is unavoidable in the context of a shared social and political community. But, in the ideal republic, no one – not any employer, not the police, not any political figure or administrative official, not any religious or community power-wielder, not any family member or work colleague – will enjoy the *unchecked* capacity to interfere in my choices.

Inevitably, in any real-world community, there will be domination to one degree or another, across every sphere. The republican state seeks to *maximise* non-domination. It strives for ever greater levels of non-domination across all aspects of the lives of all of its citizens. It seeks to empower the citizen to the point, in the ideal scenario, where she can look other citizens in the eye, and confidently assert that she enjoys resilient protection from arbitrary power. She need not 'bow and scrape' in the manner of the slave of a 'kindly master'. She can walk unafraid as an equal citizen.

So what must be in place if citizens are to enjoy this kind of liberty? There are certain familiar requirements. There must be an appropriate set of political institutions, for instance. These institutions must be designed such that power is dispersed through the polity, rather than concentrated in one individual, or in one institution. Typically, this will require a separation of powers between different arms of government: the legislature, the executive and the judiciary. In a republic worthy of the name, the executive will be accountable to the legislature in a meaningful way; in a way that ensures that people's representatives in parliament can contribute to the laws that emerge through deliberation, and can hold government to account, every day and every week, as the monotonous process of politics unfolds. Similarly, there is a need for a constitution that protects fundamental rights in the face of populist pressure. For republicans, domination by a majority group is as objectionable as domination by an individual despot.

These ingredients are well understood. They are necessary conditions for liberty, but they are by no means sufficient. Political institutions and constitutional provisions are lifeless instruments. They cannot be relied upon, on their own, to protect liberty. The political institutions cannot survive, for instance, without at least some general participation by the citizenry. There must be some kind of commitment to the democratic institutions, and at least minimal civic patriotism. Moreover, citizens must have some regard for one another, and indeed for their own status and responsibilities as citizens. There must be a general distaste for the arrogation of arbitrary power. And so on.

The point is that in order for the republican state to promote equal liberty as non-domination, it can legitimately develop virtue amongst its citizens. Indeed it *must* do so.

Civic Virtue: Do Republicans Insist on Too Thick an Account?

This presents a challenge that is of capital importance for contemporary proponents of republicanism.[2] The idea of civic virtue occupies an important place in the history of republican idealism.[3] Indeed 'civic republicanism' has often been dismissed by liberal philosophers on the ground that it sets too much store by civic virtue.[4] It is argued that republicans adopt too robust an account of virtue bearing in mind the fact that individuals living in free societies hold different reasonable world views, often radically so. Or to use John Rawls's vernacular, free societies necessarily feature a diversity of 'comprehensive doctrines': a diversity of moral, religious or philosophical 'conceptions of the good'.[5]

The argument is that republican civic virtue includes values that are 'comprehensive', and that are accordingly rejected by at least some reasonable people. Imposing a particular conception of the good on all citizens, in the form of a thick account of civic virtue, undermines the liberty of citizens who subscribe to values that differ from that account. The question might therefore be: how can republicans argue for a robust account of civic virtue, in the interests of promoting liberty as non-domination, while not going so far as to end up dominating some individuals or groups whose values clash with the account promoted?

Too many 'republics' and 'republicans' have ventured into dominating territory in this way in the past. The 2004 French law prohibiting the wearing of conspicuous religious symbols in schools, for instance, is *arguably* a dominating intervention of this kind. One justification for the prohibition, among others, was that the wearing of conspicuous religious symbols (the Islamic headscarf, effectively) in the public sphere communicated a prior loyalty to a particular religious identity, thereby intolerably undermining civic loyalty.[6] And yet the Stasi Commission (named after its chairman Bernard Stasi) deliberations that brought about the prohibition excluded the voice of Islamic women. The idea that a Muslim woman might independently choose to wear a headscarf, and that she might be simultaneously committed to the French Republic, was treated as more or less implausible. The Commission members declared themselves simply 'not sensitive to their arguments'.[7]

Another example of a dominating account of virtue – again arguably – is the attempt, orchestrated by an alliance of Eamon de Valera's Fianna Fáil and the Catholic hierarchy, to promote a particular Catholic and Gaelic, chaste and 'spurning-of-luxury' image of the ideal Irish citizen from the 1930s through much of the twentieth century.[8] This is illustrated by, for example, some provisions and the general ethos of the 1937 constitution, the official policy of conflation of civic education with Catholic social thought, and the staunch support for the control by the Catholic hierarchy over the schooling system.

There is another related argument concerning republicanism and civic virtue. This suggests that some republicans, historically, have insisted on intense political participation as the one truly 'flourishing' life.[9] They argued that human beings cannot enjoy true liberty unless they actively engage in the politics of their community, and impact directly on political deliberation and lawmaking.[10] This similarly suggests that republicanism is an inappropriate guiding philosophy for modern, ethically diverse, political communities. The citizenry of Ancient Greek city states may have had the time and means to engage in the politics of their *polis*, and, of course, citizenship was the preserve of the propertied and male elite. But many citizens of modern polities have neither the time nor the inclination. Many prefer – quite reasonably – to spend their time reading great literature, catching up on the latest celebrity gossip, or doing their best to make ends meet. Indeed, even if it were desirable, it would be simply unfeasible for all of the citizens in today's vast political communities to have a direct impact on lawmaking.

The challenge for neo-republicans, then, is to come up with an account of civic virtue that is sufficiently robust to protect equal liberty as non-domination, while not becoming so robust that it amounts to an imposition of a particular conception of the good on all citizens in circumstances where there is a deep diversity of reasonable conceptions of the good. This is quite a challenge, as the line between the un-dominating virtue and dominating imposition is a very fine one. It asks very deep questions of those seeking to defend republicanism.

The remainder of this essay is in three parts. The first part provides a broad sketch of the skills and dispositions that the state can and must develop in its young citizens. It considers the appropriate 'civic mission' of education and schooling in the modern republic, although briefly, as it is intended mainly to set up the arguments that follow. The second part is devoted to a particularly difficult challenge within the broader challenge already set out. It considers the comprehensive value of autonomy, and assesses to what extent the republican state can legitimately educate children to be independent from the ethical commitments (religious or non-religious) of their parents? These arguments then carry into the third part, which assesses the relative merits of 'common' schools and religious denominational schools in the light of this civic mission, with a particular eye on the situation in Ireland.

A Sketch of the Civic Skills and Dispositions

The legitimate civic mission of education and schooling in the modern, ethnically diverse, republic might be considered in four, closely related, categories. First, the state can promote a minimal *civic patriotism*. This should not be an overly robust or unthinking patriotism. Plainly, the temptation to present young citizens with a romantic and simplistic image of a country's history, for instance, is to be resisted. There must be a genuine effort to capture the complexity of a nation's history – and the disputes within it and about it – rather than the simplistic 'us versus them' or 'good versus evil' narrative that can all too easily prevail. Similarly, young citizens must become aware of the role and importance of the democratic institutions of the state. They must develop some commitment to these institutions, and a sense of the importance of at least minimal civic participation.

Second, young citizens must develop strong *skills of contestation*. Domination, by definition, is incontestable power. Therefore, young citizens must first be equipped with the necessary skills to identify when others enjoy arbitrary control over them (think here of the psychological impact that oppression can have over time, or the idea of 'Stockholm Syndrome'). This suggests at least rudimentary critical reasoning and autonomy-related skills. Beyond that, it suggests that they become capable of actually contesting decisions, in an appropriate and an effective way, where those decisions conflict with their interests.

Quite obviously, young citizens must develop the skills to challenge government decisions, and to contribute to the development of public policy. But dominating control can be exercised across various spheres: the political, the civic, and the private. Therefore – perhaps less obviously – young citizens must be capable of voicing their concerns and interests in the school environment, or within the clubs and associations in which they may participate. In the case of insular religious or cultural groups, for example, young members must be equipped with the skills to contest the influence of group leaders over such matters as the interpretation of religious texts or cultural traditions, and to contribute to the evolution of such interpretations. In the same vein, young people must become capable of critically assessing their own inherited religious or non-religious commitments, so that they are not permanently in thrall to those of their parents. These ideas are taken up further in the next section.

Third, the state must educate young citizens towards an appreciation of the common good of the republic as a whole, and towards an awareness of how their own private good – and the good of their families and localities – is intimately connected with that common good. Iseult Honohan argues along these lines that citizens in contemporary states must be educated towards an awareness of their 'shared common predicament and common fate' which implies that they must learn to exercise 'civic self-restraint'.[11] As Honohan suggests, rather than requiring citizens to engage in any form of political self-denial, this will require citizens to develop a deeper understanding about the ways in which their own interests are profoundly bound up in the interests of their fellow citizens. Reaching such understanding will make citizens more likely to accept, for example, redistributive economic measures to promote equality and to engage in good environmental practices.[12] In an Irish context, it would also likely counter the wretched clientelism and localism that continues to bedevil the political system.

Related to this, the state must inculcate a general distaste among young citizens for domination such that they will not seek to achieve arbitrary control over others, in the form, for instance, of excessive economic, financial or political clout, at least not for the sake of having that clout. The deeply misunderstood republican scholar Niccolò Machiavelli was particularly exercised on this point. Machiavelli lamented what he deemed the rotten factionalism among the political classes in late Middle Ages/early Renaissance Florence. The different factions sought dominating control of the levers of political power, but were motivated by their own interests, and the interests of their supporters.[13] In the Roman republic of over a millennium earlier, on Machiavelli's reckoning, different groups understood the political institutions as institutions of their own shared liberty, rather than as levers to be manipulated for personal gain.[14] The threat of being dominated by a given faction that might win power for a particular cycle led each group to secure equal liberty through good, un-dominating, non-factional laws and institutions. The idea is that citizens ought to be capable of abstracting away from their immediate whims and short-term interests, and to see the ways in which they share more valuable long-term interests in common with all citizens.

It is worth reflecting, in this context, on the extent to which the woes of post-Celtic Tiger Ireland can be attributed in great part to the excesses and the factionalism of the Celtic Tiger era. For some citizens, power-wielders and political representatives, it was about pilfering as much of the wedding cake as possible for one's own table. 'Pigs-with-their-snouts-in-the-trough' is as illuminating as any other metaphor as an illustration of Machiavelli's old argument.

Finally – and this is related to the previous point – young citizens in modern political communities must be educated towards an understanding of the 'fact of reasonable pluralism' (in John Rawls's phrase). This is the idea that an inevitable feature of any free political community is that citizens hold different moral, religious and philosophical world views, or different 'comprehensive doctrines'. More to the point, young citizens must be able to respond appropriately to the fact that they share a political community with others, many of whom hold different reasonable comprehensive doctrines. One important implication is that they must develop skills of 'public reason'.[15] For political engagement to be truly non-factional, participants in that engagement must be willing and able to offer one another non-factional (or avowable) reasons in support of their arguments in political deliberation. They must be capable of realising the unreasonableness of making arguments in political debate that are grounded only in their own deepest ethical or religious commitments.

This means that citizens must not only seek political power for more noble reasons than naked self-interest but, even more burdensomely perhaps, they must engage in the common deliberative process of politics by means of argument that they can reasonably expect their fellow citizens to accept. They cannot expect other citizens to be moved in political debate by arguments based in factional perspectives that others necessarily do not share, or by virtue of sheer political power.

Rather citizens owe one another reciprocal reasons: reasons that they can reasonably expect others not merely to understand, but to accept as legitimate.[16]

To illustrate the point, take an Irish citizen who holds Islamic beliefs, and a debate that begins (as it well might in the coming years) around the wearing of conspicuous religious insignia in public, in schools or hospitals for example. That citizen can choose between two different modes of argumentation in such a debate, along the following lines:

1. I am Islamic. Wearing the headscarf is important to me. Personally, I would fare badly if a prohibition were to be introduced. Accordingly, Ireland should not introduce a prohibition on conspicuous religious symbols.

2. All people value the norm of religious liberty. Indeed, when that norm is interpreted in a coherent way, it is as valuable to the non-religious, and to the unconventionally religious, as it is to conventional religious citizens such as myself. The right to manifest one's religious beliefs flows from that deeper norm. When the manifestation of religious belief does not undermine the equal right of others to religious liberty, it should not be restricted. Accordingly, Ireland should not introduce a prohibition on the conspicuous religious symbols.

The latter mode observes the strictures of public reason, and citizens arguing such a point might reasonably be expected to opt for it rather than for the former mode. The same kind of expectation falls on citizens from a majority ethnic or ethical group, in different debates. Catholic parents cannot argue, therefore, for a public schooling system that is run by the Catholic hierarchy, even if there is majority support for such a system (would they be happy if the atheists applied the same standards should they gain the upper hand?). Virtuous citizens living in a republic that resiliently protects them from arbitrary power can reasonably be expected to be capable of more sophisticated argumentation than the 'because-this-is-what-suits-me' kind.

This capacity for undominating democratic deliberation requires, at the very least, that young citizens be exposed to and be acquainted with other ethical perspectives, and must learn to appreciate that those other perspectives express conceptions of value that are sincerely held by other reasonable people. The beginnings of the argument concerning the relative merits of 'common' as against religious denominational schooling, which is taken up in the final section, emerge from this idea.

Educating Children Away from Inherited Beliefs: Too Much or Not Enough?

The idea that domination can be enjoyed by individuals or groups within the private sphere has already been emphasised. This section considers a particular form of domination: domination of children's ethical commitments by their parents. This quandary brings out the kernel of the dilemma: how far must a state committed to the promotion of non-domination go in educating young citizens towards virtue, and when does it go too far? When does the state begin to oppress individuals and families, in the sense of imposing an alien conception of the good on them? The starting point for any argument of this kind must be that the ethical lives of young children are the concern, first and foremost, of their parents.

While the quandary applies to all kinds of ethical commitments – religious or otherwise – it might none the less be useful to consider it in the context of a fundamentalist religious group that more or less rejects the value of autonomous ethical reflection. A helpful illustration of this dilemma is provided by a famous case that came before the US Sixth Circuit Federal Appeals Court in 1987: *Mozert v. Hawkins Co. Board of Education*.[17] The case emerged in the early 1980s from Hawkins County, Tennessee.[18] It concerned a group of Protestant religious fundamentalist parents who objected to a compulsory reading programme being taught at the public school at which their children were students. The reading programme was aimed at advancing reading skills beyond mere word and sound recognition 'to develop higher cognitive skills that [would] enable students to evaluate the material they read, to contrast the ideas presented, and to understand the complex characters that appear in the reading material'.

The parents' argument ultimately was that the reading programme exposed their children to a diverse range of ethical perspectives and encouraged 'critical reasoning', rendering it more difficult for them to pass on their particular religious beliefs to their children. They believed that it was an 'occult practice' to use the imagination beyond the limitations of scriptural authority and that exposure to secular ideas – and to religious ideas other than their own – would encourage their children to think independently about the merits of alternative ethical perspectives.

In rejecting the parents' claim, the court emphasised the civic aims of the programme. Judge Lively argued that the purpose of the public school was to teach fundamental values 'essential to a democratic society', including 'tolerance of divergent political and religious views' and the ability to 'consider . . . the sensibilities of others'. He rejected the claim that there was a violation of religious liberty on the ground that 'exposure to something does not constitute teaching, indoctrination, opposition or promotion to the things exposed'.[19]

We may agree that the *Mozert* parents are hardly representative of parents in post-Celtic Tiger Ireland, and that their objection is much more dramatic than any that is likely to emerge in that context. But their case is still illustrative. First, the same quandary applies to various degrees across the full spectrum of ethical commitments. Every parent has a particular set of ethical commitments, even if most will be much less doctrinaire than the set subscribed to by the *Mozert* parents. The set of commitments subscribed to by every parent is likely to deviate to at least some extent from whatever scheme of civic education might be promoted in a particular state. In this way, *Mozert* simply provides a particularly stark illustration of a difficulty that will be quite general across all liberal democracies. Second, while the scheme of civic education promoted in a modern republic is not likely to deviate too sharply from the ethical commitments of the majority of citizens, it might deviate quite sharply for minority groups. Hence, this quandary is all the more pressing in the light of deeper ethical heterogeneity in modern political communities.

The disputed critical reading programme in *Mozert* would seem to have pursued legitimate civic aims when judged according to republican standards. It sought to equip students with the skills and dispositions required of citizens in culturally and religiously diverse political communities. The parents objected to the manner in which the programme encouraged skills of critical reasoning, and the questioning of authority. Yet these skills are fundamental to republican citizenship,

given that their absence will bring about near absolute deference to authority, and a chronic inability to identify and
contest arbitrary power. Similarly, the lack of exposure to
alternative ethical perspectives not only tends to trap children
within their groups of origin (especially in the case of 'insular'
groups, where members tend not to mix with non-members),
but also fails to develop any sense of empathy for other perspectives. It undermines the development of any understanding of a shared political predicament and of the myriad ways
in which citizens, even in cases where ethical or religious ends
are radically different, share common interests and goods. It
seems also to conflict dramatically with the development of
even rudimentary skills of public reasoning.

And yet the scheme of civic education in *Mozert* – or the
scheme envisaged for the modern republic – seems to promote
quite forthrightly the value of autonomy. Indeed it seems
bluntly to encourage children to engage actively in critical
reflection concerning inherited ethical commitments. Rawls
argues that the value of autonomy (at least in the sense of the
active or regular scrutinising of one's ethical commitments) is
very much a 'comprehensive' one. That is, it is a value that
many individuals may embrace but, equally, that some may
reasonably reject on the basis of a preference for a life lived in
devoted and unquestioned commitment to God, for instance.
For the state to use its coercive power to promote that value,
then, is to impose a particular comprehensive doctrine on all
individuals. It is oppressive.

Rawls himself was plainly troubled by this matter. He deals
briefly with it in *Political Liberalism*, but seems conscious that
it reveals a certain incoherence at the heart of his theory of liberalism. He suggests that there might be some unfortunate
overspill from comprehensive into political liberalism, in the

sense that children educated in the way required by political liberalism might unavoidably pick up comprehensive liberal values such as that of autonomy. He concludes, somewhat perfunctorily, that 'the unavoidable consequences of reasonable requirements for children's education may have to be accepted, often with regret'.[20]

The same concern applies in the case of republicanism. If republican liberty requires a 'mission of enlightenment' of this kind, does it not veer into dominating territory? Does it breach the moral rights of parents, and lose the claim that it is an account of 'liberty'? Through the lens of the argument over civic education, a grave issue emerges for those who wish to defend republicanism as a compelling public philosophy.

Rescuing Republicanism: Distinguishing 'Ethical Independence' and 'Outright Autonomy'

So how, then, does the republican state approach these kinds of dilemmas in civic education? How does it seek to develop what appear to be crucial skills and dispositions in young citizens without being vulnerable to the charge that it is venturing into oppressive territory? Where de Valera promoted the Gaelic and God-fearing republican citizen at the cost of the liberty of those who were not so minded, contemporary republicans may make the same error in promoting the autonomous and secular citizen. This contemporary citizen is wired to engage endlessly in critical reflection on her ethical commitments. She regularly discards commitments that she no longer deems worthy, and takes them up again at a later stage when she changes her mind.

In seeking a way out of this web, it is worth recalling the essence of republicanism: it is about independence from the will of others. Indeed, republicans famously use the image of the 'kindly master' to illustrate the superiority of their conception of liberty (as non-domination) over the conception of liberty (as mere non-interference) associated with the likes of Hobbes, Mill and others.[21] The kindly master may not interfere, or be likely ever to do so, but he enjoys the *capacity* to interfere, and this brings with it the bowing and scraping, the dehumanising ingratiation of someone seeking to protect herself from interference.

This seems to shed light on Rawls's problem, and on the broader quandary in contemporary liberal democracies over civic education programmes that insist on exposure to diversity, critical reasoning skills and so on. Rather than autonomy being the issue, as such, it seems that it is independence from the will of others that is fundamntally at stake.

The image of the 'Ethically Servile' child, presented by the philosopher of education Eamonn Callan, illustrates the argument.[22] Callan does not use the language of domination, but his imagery seems to fit neatly within the republican frame. He first asks his audience to consider the example of a father of a 'Deferential Child'. The Deferential Child has been reared to believe that her duty to her father is paramount, and that her own happiness and fulfilment is contingent on her making choices that are fully at one with her father's will. The father may be totally devoted to his child's happiness and well-being – he may be the most caring father imaginable – but ultimately he is convinced that his daughter's well-being requires that she defer to him on all matters of ethical significance and so he rears her to believe that to be the case.

Callan then suggests a comparison with the 'Ethically Servile Child'.[23] This child is reared with the same goal in mind – to ensure permanent control of the child's ethical life for his understanding of her own good and happiness – but this time a different strategy is employed. Rather than rearing the child to be deferential, the father rears the child in such a way that that child will maintain an 'ignorant antipathy' towards ethical perspectives other than her inherited ethical perspectives. This notion of 'ignorant antipathy' means more than a lack of information about alternative ethical perspectives: it means a 'settled affective disposition to refuse to register whatever reason might commend in the objects of one's antipathy, even if, at some later date, one might acquire knowledge about them'.[24] The child reared towards 'ignorant antipathy' of alternative ethical perspectives is the 'Ethically Servile' child:

> Unlike the Deferential Child, my Ethically Servile Child does not think of herself as under any duty to defer to me [her parent]. She may enumerate her rights correctly, talk eloquently about their meaning, and prize them as highly as anyone reasonably could. Yet in a deep sense she remains subordinate to my will because the choices I make in moulding her character effectively pre-empt serious thought at any future date about the alternatives to my judgement. Ignorant antipathy regarding those alternatives secures her ongoing subordination in much the same way that the Deferential Child's belief that she has a duty to defer to her parents guarantees her subordination. In each case the field of deliberation in which the agent operates as an adult has been constrained through childhood experience so as to ensure ongoing compliance with another's will.[25]

Most parents, of course, would not seek to instil this kind of 'ignorant antipathy' towards other ethical perspectives in their children as a direct and self-conscious strategy. But it may be instilled, in varying degrees, subconsciously and gradually over the course of a child's upbringing. Parents, however well intentioned, cannot seek to deny their children the opportunity to become independent of their will. This is the essence of domination, with the parents as the quintessential 'kindly masters'.

By moving the analysis away from autonomy towards questions of servility, subordination and subservience to another's will, it becomes clear that any reticence among republicans in cases such as *Mozert*, or indeed about a scheme of civic education that forthrightly promotes this kind of independence for young citizens, is unjustified. The republican state cannot legitimately seek to inculcate full-blown autonomy in its young citizens, of the kind Rawls had in mind when he refers to autonomy as a comprehensive doctrine. It may not seek to instil the propensity to engage actively in intense ethical reflection such that all citizens will regularly consider which ethical commitments to continue to pursue and which to abandon. This would amount to domination by the state. But independence from the will of others is quite a different notion, and it is fundamental to republican citizenship. Republicans can forthrightly promote this good, and can legitimately call on the coercive power of the state to do so.

The point, in the end, is that the better understanding of republicanism is that which positions civic virtue appropriately, and which avoids the error of many republicans historically. If republicanism is to be compelling in the modern world, it must be a philosophy that is capable of accommodating difference and diversity. On the other side, not all 'diversity' is to be accommodated. Fundamentalist groups that reject the value of minimal autonomy, for instance, or that reject the idea of independence from the will of others, are not to be accommodated in the form of exemptions from civic education programmes that promote reasonable civic goals.[26]

The Debate Concerning Religious Denominational Schools

Finally, there is the vexed question of the relative merits of religious denominational as distinct from 'common' schooling. The question is quite urgent in Ireland, as the extent to which the Catholic Church wields control over the primary schooling system has been the subject of widespread concern in recent years. The Minister for Education, Ruairi Quinn, established the *Forum for Patronage and Pluralism in the Primary Sector* in 2011 to assess reform of the system, although the reforms proposed in the Forum's 'Advisory Report' are underwhelming.[27] Much attention has been focused on the topic over recent years, and the most striking statistic is quite familiar: more than nine out of every ten schools in the primary system are run by Catholic patrons.[28] This level of dominance straightforwardly violates the religious liberty of non-Catholics with children of school-going age all across the Irish state.[29] This section focuses on a different question: the more abstract question of whether religious denominational schools are appropriate in the light of the legitimate civic mission of education and schooling already (briefly and roughly) sketched in this essay.

Many parents want their children to be educated in schools dedicated to a particular religious ethos. These are 'sectarian' schools in the strict sense, inasmuch as they consciously promote a set of 'comprehensive' ideals. They tend to be made up of staff and students holding the same broad set of religious beliefs, and to infuse those religious beliefs into the school day and year. The 'common school', by contrast, is not defined by reference to the religious or non-religious commitments of the staff or students, nor is it dedicated to the promotion of any particular 'comprehensive' doctrine in terms of its educational ethos or mission. The common school is usually composed of teaching staff and students of different ethical perspectives, holding different religious and non-religious beliefs.

This seems to suggest, when taken at face value, that the common school is preferable in light of the civic mission of education in the modern republic. That is, it seems more likely that young students will develop attitudes of respect and empathy for citizens holding different ethical perspectives if they are educated in an environment that includes such citizens. They are more likely to develop the rudimentary skills of non-factional reasoning, and so on. This argument emerges from a simple version of the Aristotelian thesis of habituation: that 'a state of character arises from the repetition of similar activities'.[30] That is, moral character can be acquired only through active practice of the virtues; it cannot be acquired merely by abstract teaching of those virtues. If children are to be effectively segregated in their education along religious lines (or indeed along any other 'comprehensive' lines), the prospect of developing the republican skills and dispositions is undermined.

The common school, by implication, is a 'virtual republic' within which children from different cultural and religious perspectives engage with one another in a critical formative environment. They are better placed to gain an appreciation of the fact that they share a common political fate with such citizens and with all citizens in the diverse modern polity. This seems to place the onus on those arguing for religious or otherwise sectarian schools to offer strong reasons as to why they might be permitted.

Is There a Case to be Made for Religious Schools?

The first response by those wishing to defend the legitimacy (and, perhaps beyond that, the value) of religious schools to the argument as presented is that it is presented in a gravely simplistic way. It treats all 'religious' schools as if there were no important differences between institutions that fall into that broad category. Not all religious schools are 'totalistic' institutions, in which every aspect of the education they provide is determined by religious prescription. In the Irish context, although there is ample evidence of exclusion of non-Catholics in Catholic schools across the state – particularly in cases of over-subscription – it is clear that most such schools have non-Catholic staff and students, and indeed in many cases draw a considerable proportion of their membership from non-Catholics. There are deep concerns around religious liberty in these schools and in the schooling system generally, but as regards exposure to diversity and their general suitability for promoting skills and dispositions of republican citizenship, advocates of such schools are on firmer ground.

Correspondingly, the common school has often been presented in highly idealised terms, as if it necessarily features the perfect spectrum of ethical perspectives among its students and staff. The reality, of course, is that the composition of schools is more typically determined by local demographic factors and residential arrangements, and is accordingly usually much more homogenous than the ideal suggests. This would be especially true even if the common school formed the backbone of the Irish schooling system, as, despite shifts towards religious and ethical diversity over recent times, the vast majority of the population still claims to subscribe to one particular belief system.[31] (It is worth pointing out in this context that the ills of residential segregation and ghettoisation along ethnic and socio-economic lines are at least as destructive, if not drastically more destructive, to the civic mission of republican education as religious or any other kinds of sectarian schooling.)

In any case, what is clear is that the permissibility of religious schools – or indeed of any schooling environment – hinges on the question of whether such schools are willing *and able* to develop the skills and dispositions of republican citizenship. If they are, common schooling is permissible, as is home schooling, as is schooling in a school linked with a professional football club, as is schooling in a school linked with a particular religious denomination. It would seem reasonable to suggest that the common school has a significant advantage over other schooling environments, but to argue that those other environments are necessarily illegitimate is quite a jump, and probably an unreasonable one. It seems also reasonable to suggest that 'totalistic' religious schools should not be permissible.

It is critical, of course, that the republican state carefully regulates all aspects of the education and schooling environment, across all its aspects: from teacher training and pedagogy, curriculum, institutional arrangements, admissions and employment policy and so on. The difficulty of that task is clear, considering that the skills and dispositions in question are not readily amenable to quantitative assessment. Whether children are adequately protected from ethical servility, for instance, or are equipped with skills of non-factional reasoning – and whether a particular environment is or is not adequately conducive to the development of these skills – will never be straightforward.

It should also be clear that there are certain restrictions which the republican state can legitimately place on religious schools.[32] These restrictions are presented here only in abstract form. First, such schools must expose students to religious and non-religious perspectives other than the set of beliefs underpinning the school's ethos. This goal must be pursued in a genuine and comprehensive way. It must be pursued in such a way as not only to engender respect, empathy and understanding for those holding different ethical commitments, but in such a way as to present them as potentially attractive ethical lives. This will mean, at the minimum, that religious schools must be open to staff and students from outside of the endorsed faith community. Not only that, but such staff and students must enjoy their positions within those schools on an equal footing. It cannot be that they are simply tolerated, or presented as guinea pigs upon which to practise good republican virtues. On this point, the exemptions enshrined in Irish equality legislation that allow religious schools to discriminate against non-coreligionists are simply intolerable in a republic.[33]

Second, religious schools cannot incorporate religious doctrine into each and every subject in the curriculum. Although it may be permissible to teach the biblical account of creation in Religion class, for instance, it would be intolerable that that account should be taught in Biology. Similarly, there seems no good reason to incorporate religious doctrine into other classes such as History, English and so on, although it would go too far to argue that reference to religious doctrine would be impermissible.

Third, there must be a meaningful commitment across all aspects of the school to non-religious reasoning. That is, teachers must give – and insist on receiving – reasons for academic claims and rules or policies that are entirely independent of religious doctrine.[34] This will often require reasoning that conflicts with religious doctrine. Take the example of a Catholic school and questions concerning divorce, contraception or homosexuality in a class such as Social, Personal and Health Education. Although it may be permissible for students and teachers to engage in specifically Catholic argumentation on these questions, this cannot be to the exclusion of conflicting non-Catholic argumentation. Even in Religion class, the tensions within Catholicism on these questions must be thoroughly considered, as must conflicting religious and non-religious views.

In light of these arguments, it is clear that the objections to religious schooling are easily overstated. The concept of religious schooling is not necessarily in conflict with the civic mission, and so cannot be perfunctorily dismissed by republicans.

We shall never know what Machiavelli's views might have been on the question of the legitimacy of religious schooling. This essay – although drawing broadly on the tradition to which Machiavelli contributed perhaps more than anyone – has had the more modest aim of sketching a rough republican approach to civic virtue in the modern, ethically diverse, political community. Republicans need not be shy in insisting on programmes and strategies that develop independence from the will of others, including independence from the will of kindly and well-meaning parents in respect of something as sacred as their children's ethical commitments. Needless to say, the moral rights of parents to develop their children's ethical commitments must always be respected by any state committed to liberty. It is just that such rights are not absolute. And the burden is on proponents of religious schools to demonstrate that such schools are capable of educating citizens towards virtue.

5

The Law and the Republic

DEARBHAIL MCDONALD

Any debate about the law and the republic, at a time when we are asking if we still have one, invites the question as to whether the law has served or continues to serve our republic well. The surrender, in all but name, of fiscal sovereignty to the European institutions and the Sisyphean demands of 'the troika' have undermined Ireland's credentials as a republic in the hearts and minds of many of its citizens.

We are not alone among our European peers in grappling with the reality that we are no longer a self-determined state. That is if we ever truly can be a self-determined state following the gradual (then sudden) loss of sovereignty that has accompanied our largely positive membership of the European Union. Apart from the sovereignty predicament, the dawn and demise of the Celtic Tiger has led many to question the efficacy of our home-grown democratic and legal order. The extraordinary journey from boom to bust raises the question as to whether the law, in whole or in part, is somehow not fit for purpose. The purported demand for a new republic assumes that the law is not.

The fundamental design flaw at the heart of the European project (a common currency without a proper fiscal union) as well as factors such as cheap credit and regulatory failures in the financial sector, led to the near collapse of the Irish economy. And those failures, facilitated by weak and ineffectual political oversight, continue to pose a threat to our social cohesion through mass unemployment and emigration, a burgeoning mortgage and credit crisis and an ever-widening gulf between the haves and have-nots.

The dramatic bailout of many European banking systems, including Ireland's, exposed the need to develop stronger democratic institutions and a much more nuanced understanding of sovereignty and what constitutes a threat to society and the rule of law.

We know now that wrongdoing in the banking sector as well as other forms of corruption (whether negligent or malignant) in politics and business can pose as serious a threat to national security as 'ordinary' street crime and organised crime, including terrorism. The scale of disruption that followed the 2008 global economic crisis led to the introduction in Ireland of a range of emergency financial measures. These included the creation of the National Assets Management Agency (NAMA), the toxic bank that removed soured property loans from participating Irish banks, but which notably failed to offset an EU–ECB–IMF bailout in November 2010.

It also includes a series of Credit Institutions Acts, aimed, among other things, at protecting the stability of the banking system, restoring confidence in the financial sector and allowing for the orderly resolution of distressed lenders.

These laws granted extraordinary, wartime-like controls of regulation and intervention to the state, through the aegis of the Minister for Finance and the Central Bank of Ireland, over the financial system. These measures and others that followed together heralded the introduction of a special-powers regime with far-reaching consequences not seen since the time of the Troubles.

If the republic faltered in part because of a wholesale lack of regulation – a failure of the law in the broadest sense – would the birth of a new republic demand a new legal order or constitutional document? The economic crisis has understandably forced us to take stock of our mores and values, but are we at risk of overstating what went wrong in Ireland when other countries across the globe are facing similar problems? Can this crippling malaise sow the seeds for genuine constitutional and legal reform that will revive our republic or will it give birth to an entirely new one? Or are these questions themselves moot if the Irish constitution and Irish democracy are becoming mere footnotes to big country power politics?

Irish people have (historically at any rate) had an innate sense of justice, a national trait we like to think was fashioned long before the 1916 Easter Rising, the foundation of the Irish Free State in 1922 or the drafting of the 1937 Irish constitution. The writer Michael Ragan has observed that one of the reasons for the 'astounding durability' of Ireland's ancient Brehon law was the great respect that Irish natives held for justice and the law. And Sir John Davies, the British Attorney General in Ireland tasked with suppressing Brehon law, also observed that there was no nation of people under the sun that loved equal and indifferent justice better than the Irish. I wonder, given the huge socio-economic disparities in our society at present, what Sir John would make of contemporary Irish attitudes towards injustice and inequality.

Republics and the constitutions that underpin their legitimacy are typically born or recast in the wake of crises, revolutions or when, to borrow the words of T. S. Eliot, we are no longer at ease in the old dispensation. The Irish republic was itself born out of the sorry, bloody depths of the Anglo-Irish struggle. And, despite the desire for a symbolic as well as a de facto break from the British Empire, the fledgling Irish state relied heavily on that tradition for its politico-legal DNA, incorporating and maintaining much of the British parliamentary and common-law customs into the new republic. It has often been said that the Irish simply replaced the crown with a harp – once banned by the British Crown to stifle Irish rebellion – when it broke free from its former political masters. This is, in my view, a trite observation, because it ignores the dynamism inherent in Bunreacht na hÉireann, the bedrock of our republic that in 1937 replaced the 1922 constitution of the Irish Free State.

For all its faults, including a heavy reliance on Papal encyclicals and Roman Catholic teaching that has cast a long shadow on Irish politics, religion and social policy – including family, education and health – the 1937 constitution has, for the most part, proved to be a robust and innovative charter. The 1937 constitution inaugurated not just a new era of parliamentary sovereignty and representative democracy. Irish citizens also gifted to themselves a bill of fundamental rights capable of being litigated in the courts, a concept that Britain is still struggling with to this day, as its testy relationship with the incorporation and interpretation of the European Convention on Human Rights (ECHR) confirms.

The drafters also embedded the separation of powers and an express power of judicial review of legislation into the constitutional framework. The constitution itself could be changed only by way of referendum. This architecture facilitated the creation of an enduring if imperfect system of checks and balances on executive excess and granted power to judges to strike down laws deemed invalid with the provisions of the constitution. The Irish judiciary did little in the early years of the republic to heighten the fears of some of the drafters that the new constitutional contract would pave the way for un-trammelled judicial activism. But no one could have imagined that the combined phenomena of judicial review and funda-mental rights capable of being articulated and protected in court actions would lead, in time, to the creation of a host of unenumerated personal rights identified by an emboldened, liberal judiciary in landmark challenges such as *Ryan*, the famous water-fluoridation case.

Unenumerated rights are personal rights that are not expressly mentioned in legal texts such as a written constitu-tion, but are inferred, divined or carved out from existing protections or the spirit of a given document.

In an Irish constitutional context, they are unspecified rights that judges have deemed, much to the chagrin of strict opponents of judicial activism, that are implicitly guaranteed in the constitution.

In *Ryan v. Attorney General* (1965), the Supreme Court held that a water-fluoridation scheme did not infringe the plaintiff's right to bodily integrity. Critically, however, the Supreme Court found that a right to bodily integrity did exist, despite the fact that it was not explicitly mentioned in the constitution.

The landmark case established the doctrine of unenumerated rights in Irish constitutional law – that rights guaranteed by the constitution are not confined to those expressly recognised in it.

The *Ryan* case and the jurisprudence it subsequently spawned have been dogged by controversy. Not least because Mr Justice Kenny in the High Court leg of the *Ryan* case opined that this new potential tranche of unspecified personal rights – which judges would ultimately interpret – flowed from 'the Christian and democratic nature of the State'.

Cases such as *Ryan* and *McGee* (1974) which recognised a right to marital privacy – which in turn encompassed the right to use contraceptives whose importation was banned at that time – paved the way for recognition of a series of unenumerated personal rights.

Other unenumerated rights including the right of the citizen to sue the state and the right to justice and fair procedures, were subsequently divined from the constitution by judges.

These judges themselves were, it seems, inspired by their fellow jurists in the United States whose activism was attracting international acclaim. After a slow start, pioneers such as Supreme Court judge Mr Justice Brian Walsh – arguably the single most influential judge in modern Irish constitutional jurisprudence – construed the 1937 constitution as a living, breathing document where no interpretation, in Judge Walsh's own words, was 'intended to be final for all time'. And it fell to this new generation of judges, and to litigants and their lawyers who saw the potential within the constitution, to haul Irish society further into modernity than prevailing social, moral and political norms permitted.

The appetite for the kind of liberal judicial lawmaking that thrived in Ireland from the 1960s onwards did not suit all tastes. Nor did that dynamic first wave of judicial activism last. Citizens have continually tried, and failed, to persuade the courts to recognise a host of social and economic rights inherent in the constitution or to reinterpret existing personal rights in the light of new social and technological advances. Perhaps the judiciary did, on occasion, cross the constitutional line with innovative interpretations and sporadic diktats from their un-elected perches, but has the pendulum swung back too far?

It seems to me that we have, in recent years, entered into a period of entrenched, judicial conservatism where the courts –

with some notable exceptions – are loath to compel government to take any positive steps to protect citizens' rights, to identify new ones or to carve out fresh interpretations from existing rights. This may stem from a genuine and understandable fear that the separation of powers will be breached if, for example, judges are accused of directing social or economic policy from the bench or instructing the state on when and how to use its limited resources. Equally, however, the public interest is not served if the constitutional process grinds to a halt because of excessive judicial conservatism that plays into the hands of politicians unwilling to breathe life into the law and uphold their duty to legislate. It also leads to the perception that judges, more than a third of whom have direct party political or family links to legislators, are afraid to offend the political masters who appointed them.

The development of express and implied constitutional rights is not the exclusive preserve of elected representatives, who have failed abysmally to legislate in areas such as reproductive and abortion rights and family law in order to adapt to the needs of modern society. And so, some two decades after the 1992 X case that convulsed the country, we have no legal clarity on the status of the unborn or the circumstances in which women can avail of legal abortion in Ireland. Abortion has been (and remains) a criminal offence in Ireland since 1861.

But in 1983, in a pre-emptive strike against the possibility of Ireland's strict abortion regime being liberalised by judicial activism, the eighth amendment was passed to the Irish constitution. The amendment, comfortably passed, granted constutitional protection to the unborn, acknowledging as it does the equal right to life of the unborn, with 'due regard' to the equal right to life of the mother.

The fear that Ireland's criminal ban could be reviewed or liberalised by judges in part stemmed from the 1974 *McGee* decision (above) where the Supreme Court interpreted Article 40.3 of the Irish constitution as including an uneneumerated right to marital privacy and, by extension, to use contraceptives.

The eighth amendment was also motivated by factors such as the perennially controversial US Supreme Court *Roe v. Wade* ruling which recognised, on the basis of privacy law, a right to abortion in the United States of America.

In *Roe v. Wade* (1973) the US Supreme Court ruled that a right for a woman to terminate her pregnancy flowed from the right to privacy that had been established in a previous US ruling (*Griswold*, 1965), subject to the need to balance the right to life of the unborn foetus.

It was feared by some groups in Ireland that the domestic criminal ban on abortion might also be circumvented, on the grounds of privacy, by an activist Supreme Court here. Or that abortion might be liberalised courtesy of rights that might accrue to women under [then] EC law.

Designed ostensibly to placate those opposed to any relaxation of Ireland's strict abortion law, the 1983 amendment in fact laid the groundwork for an inevitable series of legal conflicts and, ultimately, the X case.

The X case, the Achilles heel of successive governments, involved a fourteen-year-old girl who became pregnant as the result of a rape. In December 1991 the girl revealed the abuse and her pregnant state to her parents and, after discussion, it was agreed that she should travel to England for an abortion.

When the distressed teenager's parents contacted the Gardaí (Irish police) to inquire if DNA evidence extracted from the aborted foetus could be used as evidence against her abuser, Gardaí contacted the Office of the Director of Public Prosecutions. The DPP, in turn, contacted the then Attorney General Harry Whelehan SC who obtained a High Court injunction preventing X from travelling abroad to terminate her pregnancy.

The resulting publicity about the injunction and X's plight proved extremely divisive and placed the courts in the unenviable if impossible role of balancing the equal right to life of the mother and her unborn foetus.

The High Court upheld the injunction, but the Supreme Court discharged it, mindful as members of the court were of the contention that there was a real and imminent risk that X would commit suicide if forced to proceed with her pregnancy.

In its ruling, the Supreme Court inisted that it was not for the courts to programme society and the late Supreme Court judge Mr Justice Niall McCarthy berated the government for its 'inexcusable' failure to introduce appropriate laws with regard to abortion.

In the end, the Supreme Court came up with a formula that allowed X to travel, although tragically she later had a miscarriage. The formula led to the recognition of legal abortion in Ireland, albeit in highly limited circumstances. As a result of X, abortion is permissible in Ireland if it is established as a matter of probability that there is a real and substantial risk to the life – as distinct from the health – of the mother which can be avoided only by the termination of the pregnancy.

This risk to maternal health includes the risk of suicide. But the formula angered many, not least because some questioned what evidence would be required to establish a threat to a mother's life (including a risk of suicide) and also because the court's formula did not place any time limits on when a termination could take place.

Since X, there have been numerous abortion-related referendums and a heartbreaking alphabet soup of cases brought in Ireland and before the European Court of Human Rights (ECtHR) by women seeking – among other things – for the law, post-X, to be clarified.

It has yet to be clarified and I often wonder what X, born in the same year as I was, must think of that landmark case now.

For Irish society, the abortion issue seems intractable: for elected representatives, it is political suicide. But that difficulty does not, as Judge McCarthy highlighted all those years ago, excuse our politicians from failing to legislate.

The X vacuum has had significant consequences for related areas such as IVF treatment, surrogacy and embryo research where medical advances alone, not to mention changes in attitudes over time, have demanded fresh legal and moral responses. This political dereliction of duty, coupled with a kind of judicial cowardice, has forced citizens, increasingly, to look outside the state, to bodies such as the ECtHR to safeguard civil and political rights that should find a domestic remedy within the body and spirit of our constitution and national body of laws.

Most citizens' lives are far removed from the often elitist debates about Irish constitutional jurisprudence, and the law is much more than a single document or set of rules. I spend much of my working life in the Four Courts and the Criminal Courts of Justice, less frequently at the Circuit and District Courts, even though this is where the vast majority of citizens interact with the legal system. From that vantage point you get to see the very best in Irish legal practice, including world-class advocacy and lawyers willing to take on unpopular or hopeless cases, often for no fee. You see the work of judges who are fair, fearless and independent, compassionate too in their rulings and the exercise of their wide-ranging discretion. On occasion you see glimpses of the worst in human behaviour and I have been genuinely shocked and saddened at the manner in which a small number of judges address citizens and non-nationals alike, who are treated in a summary and dismissive manner. Citizens have little or no recourse if they are unhappy with the way in which they have been treated in court, as distinct from appealing a decision on a point of law or the merits of a case. It is at times like this that I think of our forefather Brehon judges, whose traditional badge of office was a torque worn around their necks, which reputedly tightened if they lied or delivered an unfair or biased ruling. Their cheeks would blotch out of fear that they would be made personally liable for damages – or lose their jobs.

What about judicial ethics and conduct in this republic? More than ten years have passed since the Sheedy affair, which led to the resignation of two senior judges.

In 1999, Supreme Court Judge Hugh O'Flaherty and his High Court colleague Judge Cyril Kelly resigned after a Dublin man, Philip Sheedy, had the remainder of a four-year jail sentence suspended after serving one year. Mr Sheedy, an architect, had been convicted of dangerous driving causing death and the circumstances surrounding his early release prompted calls for a mechanism to allow judges' conduct to be subject to review.

The Judge Brian Curtin controversy also still sticks in the craw. In 2004 Circuit Court judge Brian Curtin was acquitted on on alleged child-pornography charges. The jury was directed to acquit Judge Curtin when it was revealed that

Gardaí had seized his computer illegally on an out-of-date search warrant. The judge later resigned after the government moved to impeach him.

In the wake of the Sheedy affair, the former Chief Justice Mr Justice Ronan Keane compiled a report that recommended the establishment of a judicial council with specific powers to conduct inquiries into allegations concerning the conduct of judges. The government is finally moving in this direction. So too is the judiciary, which – in what some viewed as a pre-emptive strike – has set up its own representative council, the Association of Judges of Ireland (AJI).

The relationship between the executive and the judiciary has, like many relationships, been strained by the economic crisis. The failed Oireachtas Inquiries Referendum, which planned to grant powers to politicians hold inquiries – but left doubt as to whether those being inquired into could access the courts if they believed their rights were being infringed – led to concerns that politicians were trying to take power back from judges. The flawed wording itself reflected the frustration of many politicians who resort to grandstanding because of a weak parliamentary edifice, copper-fastened by the whip system that emasculates them. It reflected a system that allows the Seanad, our upper house, to function as a nursery cum retirement home for party apparatchiks instead of a vital check on the executive and parliament. It is a system that lacks a strong independent committee system, as in Britain or the United States, to facilitate the formulation of policy in an inclusive and considered manner instead of allowing laws to be executed by guillotine.

In short, it is a system that – to our shame – has reduced our politicians to sheep, rather than the statesmen many aspire to be. Those weaknesses, and the overarching dominance of the executive, need to be addressed as part of any discussion about a new republic. But not, I would suggest, at the expense of an independent judiciary, without which there is no democracy.

The referendum to overturn the constitutional ban on reducing judges' pay while in office provided another source of antagonism between the executive and the judiciary. The seed for the success of the referendum to reduce judges' pay was sown by judges themselves. The bench scored a spectacular own goal when judges failed to sign up as a group to a voluntary scheme with the Revenue Commissioners in lieu of a mandatory pension levy for all public servants. Most, in time, did so, but the gesture was not sufficient to appease the citizenry's wrath. The referendum to reduce judges' pay was an easy one to pass, tapping as it did into the populist urge to force well-paid judges with lucrative pensions to take a pay cut. But the *raison d'être* for the former constitutional ban, to ensure politicians would not target judicial earnings at a whim – and that judges would not feel pressurised to placate their political paymasters – was largely lost in the debate.

Now we have a situation where judges, unelected and virtually unimpeachable, are dealing directly with government – with no independent body to intervene – on issues of pay, pensions and other matters that the public may never become aware of. This is the potentially dangerous scenario the original constitutional ban sought to ensure would never happen.

Added to this mix is our outdated and unsatisfactory system of appointing judges. Notwithstanding the introduction, in 1995, of the Judicial Appointments Advisory Board – a body established to depoliticise the judicial appointments process – judges are still political appointees, and this carries a risk, however small, of undue influence by the executive.

More damning than the risk, however small, of undue influence by the executive is the public perception that politicians are packing the courts with political appointees.

Any assessment of whether the law is serving the republic requires an examination of some or all of the fundamentals that are said to define a republic. One of the grounding principles is access to justice. At present, vast numbers of citizens are denied access to justice owing to a range of factors, including inexcusable delays in court procedures that could be diminished by simple structural reforms and targeted investment. The creation of the Commercial Court, which was set up to fast-track big-business disputes and make Ireland an attractive place for corporations, is one excellent example of how the state can facilitate access to justice when it needs to.

The prohibitive legal cost of going to court is arguably the biggest barrier to seeking justice. It seems that only the very rich or the very poor, with everything to gain or nothing to lose, can have their day in court or afford the independent legal advice they need to assert and protect their rights. Access to civil legal aid is woefully insufficient and is a major barrier to ordinary members of the public getting access to the courts and legal representation. And for those living on the bread line deemed lucky enough to qualify for the scheme, they have to endure a chronically long waiting time, which only adds to the injustice. A key role is now being played by a host of non-governmental organisations such as the Free Legal Advice Centres (FLAC) and the Northside Community Law Centre (NCLC) who are stepping into the breach to provide access to justice for those on the margins of society and the new 'working poor' struggling to deal with mortgages and personal debts.

The surge in demand for these services and recourse to state agencies such as the Legal Aid Board and the Money Advice and Budgeting Service (MABS) – notwithstanding the excellent services under difficult circumstances these bodies provide – is not a cause for celebration: it is a damning indictment of the state's failure to provide access to justice for the bulk of its citizens.

The issue of legal costs has been shamefully kicked into touch by both the legal profession and the government, which – as the largest single buyer of legal services – bears a huge responsibility for allowing costs to spiral and maintaining them at artificially high levels. Separately, a somewhat disturbing campaign has been mounted against the criminal legal-aid scheme, arguably the one part of the criminal-justice system that works quite well. Successive governments have introduced a range of legislative measures encroaching on the custodial and pre-trial rights of accused persons who are almost exclusively drawn from Ireland's lowest socio-economic ranks.

Efficiencies can always be improved and the criminal legal-aid scheme is not immune from abuse. But it seems obscene and disproportionate to be attacking underclasses that need the financial assistance of the state in order to fight the extensive resources of the state – especially at a time when more than €260m a year is being paid to legal panels hired by NAMA to carry out due diligence on loans that should have been carried out by lawyers and the banks they worked for in the first place. It is worth dwelling on the fact that some €2.6bn or more has been earmarked to cover legal and related fees in connection with the various transactions that will take place over the projected ten-year lifespan of the Kafkaesque agency whose inner workings are shielded in secrecy. This is money that will be spent on lawyers and others to clean up the failure to regulate our banks. In comparison, the criminal legal-aid scheme costs less than €60m a year – and this amount is in steep decline. The cost of running the Office of the Director of Public Prosecutions is still less at some €40m a year.

It is not the fault of the legal profession that the banks almost collapsed, although the legal sector and other professions certainly had a role to play. But if the €85bn price that current and future generations must pay has its roots in a wholesale lack of regulation, at heart a catastrophic failure of the law, then the law did not serve the republic well: it almost destroyed it. What is even more galling, and without prejudice to the many investigations that are under way into the activity of individuals at certain financial institutions and elsewhere, is the fact few people have been charged, let alone convicted, in relation to the near collapse of the economy. And yet we continue to send thousands of people to jail every year over their failure to pay civil debts such as credit cards, credit-union arrears, dog and television licences, while leaving high-flying tax evaders – including elected representatives – at large and free from prosecution.

This two-tier justice system is deeply corrosive. It undermines society's faith in the prosecution of white-collar crime and is an affront to social solidarity and the republican ideal of equality. And despite the need to reform radically the legal profession and the system it serves, I doubt whether the proposed Legal Services Regulation Bill (LSRB) will address many of the critical issues facing ordinary members of the public seeking access to justice.

There are many ways in which citizens can be denied access to justice. The destruction of much of our human-rights infrastructure, including the Irish Human Rights Commission and the Equality Authority, is one such example. The filleting of the Freedom of Information regime is another. One of my own personal bugbears is the operation of the In Camera rule that cloaks all family law and almost all childcare proceedings in privacy. The case for a considered relaxation of the In Camera rule in family law proceedings and proceedings involving children is overwhelming. It has been for some time. The blanket ban enshrined in the Courts (Supplemental Provisions) Act 1961 and reiterated across several statutes including our divorce, domestic violence and childcare laws, is designed to protect the privacy of families and children embroiled in family and child law cases. But the blanket nature of the ban is a disproportionate measure, an insult to the constitutional principle of open justice and is unfair to families seeking justice in the courts. No one expects the veil of secrecy to be lifted entirely in family and child law cases, but it should be pierced sufficiently to enhance public confidence in the family law courts to promote the type of public debate that, in turn, will lead to better-informed social and legal policies in this area. The bar is raised even further in childcare proceedings. The treatment of children in care is a matter of public law in the broadest sense and, all too often, the need to protect the identity of troubled children coincides with the need to protect the system that is failing them. Given the competing constitutional rights at stake, any reform of the In Camera rule must be measured, but it must be done.

Another issue to be addressed in this period of post-crisis reflection is how far threats such as terrorism or financial emergency can be used to justify encroachments on our civil liberties and personal rights. This is the cry of emergency, which Supreme Court judge Mr Justice Adrian Hardiman described in the constitutional challenge against NAMA by property investor Paddy McKillen as an 'intoxicating one, producing an exhilarating freedom from the need to consider the rights of others and productive of a desire to repeat it again and again'.

There are legitimate situations in which the rule of law must be suspended or subdued to meet a crisis. The present constitution identifies these situations as a state of armed war or rebellion. The rule of law can also be set aside in times of natural disaster or in an acute public-health crisis. And it is accepted, in a country that introduced special powers to stand down subversive activity during the Troubles, that terrorism and gang-related crime could test the rule of law to its limits and require legitimate responses.

One of the reasons, I suspect, why there have been calls in some quarters to reimagine a new republic stems in part from the abuse of the cry of emergency by the executive in recent years, including crucial decisions such as the now discredited banking guarantee issued in 2008 without any democratic discussion of its consequences.

The night of the bank guarantee, involving as it did the convening of an 'incorporeal' cabinet meeting in the wee small hours as Gardaí were sent to the home of a sleeping government minister, continues – in the absence of transparency surrounding the circumstances leading up to the all-encompassing guarantee – to cause huge offence and suspicion. This at a time when public confidence in the political system, debased by lasting images of politicians and developers frolicking in the tent at the Galway Races, has been decimated.

The public's reaction to the present crisis and its origins resembles, at times, much of the caustic rage expressed during the notorious Dublin Lockout by the Irish poet William Butler Yeats in his seminal poem 'September, 1913', in which Yeats castigates those in power who do not do right by the citizens of Ireland.

Almost a hundred years after Yeats's searing attack on the political and merchant classes, Irish citizens are suffering from what might be described as a lockout syndrome. Many look with contempt on the political as well as the banking, corporate and legal classes. They hold those classes, with their light-touch regulation, responsible for 'fumbling in a greasy till' during the good times and drying marrow from the bones of the poor and new working poor during the current recession.

This is not to say that the politicians and civil servants tasked with dealing with the economic crisis have not faced tough choices and many, no doubt, hold a sincere belief that they acted in the public interest. But the executive has failed to justify to the public many of the emergency measures and the unreviewable powers it granted to itself and to external agencies such as the European Central Bank. All too often, the emergency measure becomes normalised and, when that happens, democracy and the rule of law are the real losers. That is one of the reasons why, I imagine, so many citizens feel powerless.

This loss of sovereignty, more real than imagined, is fuelling demand for a new republic, a reordering of our democracy. And that leads us to the big white elephant in the room: Europe. It is simply not possible to contemplate a new republic or constitution without considering the future of Europe, that still unfolding drama. There are so many tough questions we must ask as we harbour hopes of a new republic.

How far are we prepared to go to alter our society radically? Can the constitutional supremacy of the family based on marriage be maintained in light of the changing nature of Irish families? Should we extend full marital rights to gay and lesbian couples as part of a true equality agenda? Should a new constitution incorporate meaningful social and economic rights such as the right to housing and healthcare? Is a new constitution enough to renew our democracy and do we have the guts to back our aspirations up with radical institutional reform to give life to our ideals?

But these questions, and many like them, seem redundant when compared with Ireland's awesome loss of sovereignty engendered by the financial crisis, as well as the debate about the future of Europe and Ireland's role within it. The fiscal treaty referendum, and the Lisbon Treaty before it, was passed out of fear, voters ticking yes from the confines of their fiscal straitjackets. Other countries have experienced social unrest as a consequence of the imposed austerity programme, but the Irish population it seems has been cowed into submission.

The big questions, such as under what law was the transfer of resources from current and future generations of Irish citizens to French and German bondholders mandated, are not being asked. Questions such as which European constitution or rule requires the ECB to account to Irish citizens are not being raised because of a fear of jeopardising the chance of future bailouts. Few are asking how the Irish state and other small democracies at the periphery of Europe can truly protect their citizens when their authority and the constitutions from which they derive their power are incidental to the main European drama. The silence that follows these questions speaks volumes about the health of our republic and the difficulties of imagining a new one.

The Herculean debate we need to have around sovereignty, the core of any republic, also makes a mockery of the government's planned Constitutional Convention. The 'comprehensive constitutional reform' to be discussed, including lowering the voting age by a year and reducing the presidential term by two years, is wholly inconsequential compared to the fundamental debates around sovereignty and electoral reform we badly need.

The task of reimagining a new republic, therefore, will not be an easy one, but the role of the law will be critical to that task. The law, like life, is relentless and must move forward. And the law will be one of the most important components of any reordered republic as it will hold up – as it does now – a mirror to our heritage and values. Any new republic will necessarily have to incorporate a new legal order, but how much of the old republic would we discard? I imagine that if we did imagine a new republic, if we rewrote the Irish constitution, much of the spirit and substance of the 1937 document would survive the transition to a new sovereign order. In doing so, we can find inspiration in our rich legal ancestry and the community-based ethos much loved by the ancient Irish. Yeats summonsed the ghosts of John O'Leary, Edward Fitzgerald, Robert Emmet and Wolfe Tone, patriots who sacrificed themselves so that Ireland could be a great nation. Is Romantic Ireland truly dead and gone; can we prove Yeats wrong? A new republic will require brave revolutionaries of the kind who are willing to stand up for Ireland's best interests and honour the plight of our new 'wild geese' disenchanted or exiled by the economic crisis.

6

Citizens or Subjects? Civil Society and the Republic

FRED POWELL

Saturday 3 December 2011 saw a hugely successful pre-budget 'Parade of Defiance' against the IMF-imposed cuts throughout the streets of Cork. This was a creative protest organised by *Occupy Cork* to show the city's opposition to austerity measures and to raise our voices together against the undemocratic forcing of these cuts on the people of this country. Between 1,000 and 1,200 people marched behind banners with messages such as 'Not my Debt' and 'This is not a Recession, this is a Robbery'.

Occupy Cork, issue 3, 2011

The Little People came suddenly. I don't know who they are. I don't know what it means. I was a prisoner of the story [*IQ84*]. I had no choice. They came, and I described it. That is my work.

Haruki Murakami,
New York Review of Books, 8 December 2011

Two recent events captured the essence of our times. First, the Occupy movement which began in Wall Street, New York City, on 17 September 2011, and spread across the world. The message of the Occupy movement is a simple one. It opposes the austerity measures imposed on ordinary people around the world, the 99 per cent who it argues have been expropriated by the wealthiest 1 per cent of the population. Second, the much anticipated Haruki Murakami novel was published in 2011, entitled *IQ84*. Clearly inspired by George Orwell's *1984* parable about Stalinist tyranny, *IQ84* takes the reader into a counterworld of unreality. Surveillance is all-pervasive and the innocent 'Little People' hide from a weirdly unsettling Lewis Carroll wonderland of horrors and the horrifying exercise of power over the mesmerised. Both the Occupy movement and Murakami's *IQ84* illuminate aspects of the world we currently inhabit: the dominance of unaccountable and largely invisible systems of power but also the willingness of citizens to struggle against these dark forces. The 'Little People' have become the 'unsignified signifiers' probing behind the mirror of power.[1]

This essay is about the meaning of civil society and its relevance to the idea of 'The Republic' in the conditions of economic and political crisis that define twenty-first-century Ireland. It is also about the relationship between fiction and reality in our contemporary political narrative. It offers, finally, ten principles for critical citizenship.

Civil Society, Rights and Democracy

In the debate about civil society the key terms – civil/civic, society, virtue, community – all originate in the ancient world. For our purposes however, the debate in the modern world is traceable to the Enlightenment. Key early influences were Thomas Hobbes (1588–1679), John Locke (1632–1704) and Benedict de Spinoza (1632–1677). Hobbes and Locke constructed civil society 'as a contractually produced and politically guaranteed instrument of individuals who came together to attain some conscious purpose'.[2] Spinoza rejects Hobbes's conservative contractarianism as too negative in terms of constraining human freedom, most prominently in the latter's book *Leviathan* (1651). He similarly rejects Locke's more liberal reformulation of Hobbes. Instead Spinoza presents liberty 'as a positive good or inalienable potential', in which political freedom can flourish and where reason and virtue are connected in a benevolent relationship between the citizen and the state.[3] The logic of Spinoza's argument is fundamentally radical. Russ Leo asserts 'it is Spinoza and Spinozism which promotes the adoption of secular reason and government, universal toleration and shared equity among all men, personal liberty, freedom of expression and democratic republicanism'.[4] Conservatives rejected 'Spinozist claims as anarchic and atheistic innovations that quickly breach the limit of what is necessary to maintain order, and morality in a civil (and religious) society'.[5] Despite censorship and police surveillance 'by the mid-1670s Spinoza stood at the head of an underground radical philosophical movement rooted in the Netherlands but decidedly European in scope'.[6]

After Spinoza's death in 1677 a 'forbidden movement' inspired by his ideas spread across Europe despite the constraints of censorship, suppression and hostility.[7] Liberal thinkers of more moderate persuasion also began to explore the importance of civil society – notably in Scotland. The Scottish Enlightenment sought to resolve the relationship between faith and reason through Scottish Common Sense, which put it at odds with the Radical Enlightenment of Spinozism.[8] *The Theory of Moral Sentiments* (1759) by Adam Smith (1723–1790) 'offered a powerful conjecture about the way in which some citizens acquire that sense of fitness and ethical beauty which makes it possible for them to aspire to a life of virtue'.⁹ John Ehrenberg concludes 'it was Adam Smith who first articulated a specifically bourgeois conception of civil society. His effort to integrate economic activity and market processes in a more general understanding of the anatomy of civilized life is a milestone in the development of modern thought.'¹⁰ The explicit use of the term is first evident in a treatise by the Scottish Enlightenment thinker, Adam Ferguson, who first published *An Essay on the History of Civil Society* in 1773. In this work Ferguson explores the tensions and paradoxes inherent in the concept of civil society, which persist to the present day.

Similarly the German philosopher, Georg Wilhelm Friedrich Hegel (1770–1831), explored the concept of civil society in the definitive version of his monumental system of political and social philosophy, as it appeared in the 1821 edition of *Philosophy of Right*. For Hegel, civil society incorporates the spheres of economic relations and class formation as well as the judicial and administrative structure of the state. He does not include pre-state relations, such as the family and community, which essentially define the term 'civil society' in its most common usage today.

The debate about civil society in modern social and political thought started in the Old World, but quickly crossed the Atlantic to the New World of the American Colonies. Essential to the widening of the debate was Thomas Paine (1737–1809), raconteur, polemicist and republican, who dominated progressive political thought in Britain, France, America and Ireland during the age of revolutionary struggle against absolutist tyranny in the last quarter of the eighteenth century. In his highly influential pamphlet, *Common Sense*, published in 1776, Paine introduced the term 'civilised society' as a natural and potentially self-regulating form of association, counterpoised to 'Government', which was in his view, at best, a necessary and artificial evil. However, Paine was vague about what precisely he meant by civil society.[11] Paine's radical republicanism spread to Ireland and proved a formative influence on the United Irishmen.[12] His pamphlet *Rights of Man* sold 40,000 copies in Ireland.[13]

The French aristocrat Alexis de Tocqueville (1805–1859), who visited the United States in the 1830s, was a great deal more cautious. Liberal by political persuasion, de Tocqueville is sometimes regarded as having depoliticised the term 'civil society', celebrating any form of associational activity for its own sake in his study *Democracy in America*, first published in 1835. In fact, de Tocqueville laid considerable stress on participation in local democracy as the best method for ensuring that civil association reinforced and protected democratic politics against tyranny. However, the core of his conception of civil society devolved on the health of intermediate institutions, usually the family, the community and churches. As de Tocqueville put it:

> Amongst the laws which rule human societies, there is one which seems to be more precise and clear than all others. If men are to remain civilised, or to become so, the art of associating together must grow and improve in the same ration in which equality of conditions is increased.[14]

Howard Zinn[15] in his classic study *A People's History of the United States* has cast doubt on de Tocqueville's positive vision of American civil society, arguing that it was in reality profoundly divided between rich and poor. De Tocqueville's cautious liberalism was to prove highly influential on the Young Ireland movement during the 1840s.[16]

While de Tocqueville was commenting from the perspective of liberal individualism other contemporary thinkers addressed the concept of civil society from a very different ideological standpoint. Utopian Socialists, including Henri de Saint-Simon (1760–1825), Charles Fourier (1772–1837) and Etienne Cabet (1788–1856), saw the great sources of evil in society as cut-throat competition, deceit, greed and inhumanity, and the great remedy as association and co-operation to restore harmony to human life. Fourierist communities, based on the ideals of association and co-operation, were established in New Jersey, Wisconsin and Massachusetts. In Ireland Robert Owen (1771–1858) and William Thompson (1775–1833) advocated similar ideals. Thompson's co-operativist ideals led to the establishment of the Ralahine community in early nineteenth-century Ireland.

On the other hand, Karl Marx (1818–1883), who along with a group of fellow German refugees in Paris in 1832 established the League of the Just (later the Communist League) as a bulwark against capitalism, rejected civil society. Marx regarded 'civil society as an illusion that needs to be unmasked'.[17] Later Marxists, notably Antonio Gramsci (1891–1937), who struggled against fascist tyranny in twentieth-century Italy, reworked the Marxist position. In his *Prison Notebook*, commenced in 1929 at the beginning of a twenty-year prison sentence, Gramsci wrote:

> What we can do, for the moment, is to fix two major superstructural 'levels': that one can be called 'civil society', and that of 'political society' or the 'State'. These two levels correspond on the one hand to the

function of 'hegemony' which the dominant group exercises throughout society, and on the other hand to that of 'direct domination' or rule exercised through the State and the judicial Government.[18]

For Gramsci, social inequality and class domination were exercised by a variety of cultural institutions that enabled the dominant group to impose its sense of reality on the rest of society. It was only through addressing the labyrinthine cultural complexity that the oppressed could liberate themselves and wrest control of civil society from the bourgeoisie, which had traditionally opposed popular participation. In Gramscian terms civil society was conceived as the site of alternative hegemonies.

From Gramsci's perspective the revolutionary task was not about the Jacobin–Leninist seizure of power, its inevitable violence and totalitarian outcome, with 'the Party becoming the Prince'. Political rupture in Gramsci's theory of action was about a struggle to liberate human consciousness from hegemonic domination. There is a direct link between Spinoza and Gramsci in their emphasis on a 'revolution of the mind', as a prelude to and condition of human freedom. Both sought to address existing hegemonies of power.

Gramsci had fundamentally changed Marx's economic determinism by adding culture to the cause of revolutionary change. In doing so he opened the way for a radical civil society, based on gender, ethnicity, sexuality, disability and environment to flourish during the second half of the twentieth century. New social movements have created a democratic force 'from below' that has revived the Ancient Greek tradition of civic republicanism based upon the *agora* – as a gathering place or citizen's assembly.

However, as Chris Hann and Elizabeth Dunn observe, 'it is the liberal strand that has become almost hegemonic in most recent debates'[19] about civil society. This is most obviously due to the transformation of Eastern Europe during the 1980s that brought about the overthrow of Stalinist tyranny. A more profound and subtle influence has been the universalisation of Western notions of freely associating individuals in a pluralistic democratic society, which have become the dominant political paradigm in postmodern society. Postmodernity represents the replacement of standardisation, nation states and uniformity that characterised the modern era by fragmentation, globalisation and the affirmation of individual difference.

While the struggles of Eastern European dissidents, most famously the Czech playwright Vaclav Havel, highlighted the threat to civil society in state-dominated regimes, there is a growing sense of the complexity of issues in postmodern society. Havel, later installed as the President of the Czech Republic following the Velvet Revolution, argued for 'anti-political politics'. Subsequently, a more sober analysis has emerged of the tide of change sweeping Eastern Europe since 1989. Hann and Dunn have observed that:

> The recent revolutions in Eastern Europe were the first in human history not to be concerned with establishing some form of rational Utopia. These societies (post-communist) are seen as characterised by unfettered egoism and consumerism. Only individuals exist, and they are allegedly devoid of significant human relationships.[20]

Vladimir Putin's Russia is manifestly democratically compromised and challenged by its internal critics. His suppression of civil society is also undemocratic.[23]

The equation of civil society with a generic Euro-American state is clearly an ideological position that has more to do with post-Cold War politics than serious social analysis. There are, manifestly, various definitions of civil society in the history of social and political thought, as outlined above. But the core distinction is probably a lexical conflict of meanings inherent in the term 'civil society', between 'citizen society' and 'market society'. This ambiguity is apparent in the German term for civil society, *burgerliche Gesellschaft*, translatable as both 'citizen society' and 'bourgeoisie society'.

Jean L. Cohen and Andrew Arato[24] have demonstrated how these two counterpoised meanings might be harmoniously reconciled without either becoming dominant over the other. They advocate a three-part model of social structure differentiating between (1) the activities of commerce, (2) the administrative powers of the state and (3) civil society that fosters a vibrant lifeworld of symbols and solidarities. Cohen and Arato consequently define civil society as 'a sphere of social interaction between economy and State, composed above all of the intimate sphere (especially the family), the sphere of associations (especially voluntary associations), social movements, and forms of public communications . . . institutionalised and generalised through laws'.[25]

The definition offered by Cohen and Arato creatively avoids conceptual ambiguity. But deeper, longer-term historical issues are also at stake. While much of the current social condition is novel, there is clearly an ongoing debate about the nature of society and the role of the individual. The debate about civil society is emblematic of this more fundamental debate in an age when the grand historical narrative (Christianity, Marxism, and so on) has lost its persuasive force, at least in Western society. The replacement of the modern project of the nation state, latterly the welfare state, by 'post-modernity' raises larger questions about the idea of civil society to which we must now turn.

Political Language, Truth and Power

Civil society is politically about humanity's desire to nurture a public sphere for the common good. But there political contestation begins. Truth is shaped by ideology. Because we live in an era when conservatism is once again in the ascendant, we should not be blinded by its truths. The 2005 Nobel Laureate for Literature, Harold Pinter, reminded the world in his acceptance speech that 'there are many truths', adding that 'these truths challenge each other, recoil from each other, reflect from each other, tease each other'. He observed in relation to power and truth:

> Political language, as used by politicians, does not venture into any of this territory since the majority of politicians, on the evidence available to us, are interested not in truth but in power and in the maintenance of that power. To maintain that power it is essential that people remain in ignorance of the truth, even the truth of their own lives. What surrounds us therefore is a vast tapestry of lies, upon which we feed.[26]

Pinter concluded: 'Sometimes you feel you have the truth of the moment in your hand then it slips through your fingers and is lost.'[27] These wise observations on the many-sided nature of truth underline the complexity of the task of understanding civil society in political terms. That a great seer of Pinter's stature should find the truth so challenging underlines the task for us lesser mortals. He has posed profound questions about the quality and reality of our democratic experience. Civil society has a key role in monitoring democracy.[28]

Strong Democracy: Beyond Political Zoology

Benjamin Barber in his book *Strong Democracy*, published in 1984, laments the erosion of democracy from within, through the triumph of thin (representative) democracy – which in his view marginalises citizens from the decision-making process. He likens this process to 'politics as zookeeping', in which 'democracy is undone by a hundred kinds of activity more profitable than citizenship; by a thousand seductive acquisitions cheaper than liberty'.[29] Thin democracy shifts power to distant representative institutions, far from communities where citizens live. Instead of participation in decision-making, citizens are reduced to a passive state like animals in a zoo waiting for their keepers to decide their lives for them. Strong democracy envisages the participation of all the citizenry in at least some aspects of governance at least some of the time. Civil society opens up the public realm to the possibility of participative democracy. As Barber puts it:

> From the perspective of this political zoology, civil society is an alternative to the 'jungle' – to war of all against all that defines the state of nature. In that poor and brutish war, the beasts howl in voices made articulate by reason – for zoos, for cages and trainers, for rules and regulations, for regular feeding times and prudent custodians. Like captured leopards, men are to be admired for their unshackled freedom, but they must be caged for their untrustworthiness and anti-social orneriness all the same.

Indeed, if the individual is dangerous, the species is deadly. Liberal democracy's sturdiest cages are reserved for the People.[30]

Strong democracy offers society the choice of taking responsibility for the democratic restoration that has the potential to give substance to the somewhat hackneyed slogan 'power to the people'.

Thomas Prugh et al. assert:

Strong democracy offers several immediate advantages over current systems:

- It would make communities stronger and more reflective of their residents' visions for their common lives. Strong democracy builds community by engaging people with each other as they struggle to address common issues. It strengthens the 'us' without sacrificing the 'me'.
- Strong democracy disperses power, redistributing it downward so that governance is less susceptible to dominance by specific interests.
- Strong democracy acts as a reality check by bringing citizens more directly into contact with the problems of governance.[31]

They add: 'We need a politics of engagement, not a politics of consignment, in other words participative rather than representative democracy.'[32]

We live in a world where many active citizens are concerned to address the democratic deficits that have arisen in the period of globalisation. Participation has become a pivotal concern.

Iris Marion Young asserts that 'beyond membership and voting rights, inclusive democracy enables participation and voice for all those affected by problems and their proposed solutions'.[33] In essence, this is a statement of strong democracy. It promotes participation and inclusion. In contrast, thin democracy leaves it to political elites to speak for us and represent our interests. There is a fundamental issue of political equality and republican respect at issue here. Moreover, there is an issue of trust and toleration that defines pluralistic democracy. The reality is that not everybody is given equal voice in liberal democratic societies. Monarchy survives in its exalted role as a wholly undemocratic institution based on the most extreme form of exclusion – blood lineage. But perhaps more troubling is the role of the oligarchies of power and wealth in manufacturing consensus, through their capacity to monopolise the media and purchase political influence. In this hierarchal world of power, exclusion is rife. As Young puts it, 'perhaps the most pervasive and insidious form of external exclusion in modern democracies is what I referred to as the ability for economically or socially powerful actors also to exercise political domination'.[34] She asserts that 'one task of democratic civil society is to explore and criticise exclusions such as these, and doing so sometimes effectively challenge the legitimacy of institutional rules and their decisions'.[35] The above critique of the limits of democratic inclusion invites the question, 'Is there any point in participation?' Bill Cooke and Uma Kothari (2002) suggest that there might not be any value in participation and add that it is unreasonable to push people in that direction.[36] They view the postmodern political landscape as barren and civil society as a meaningless concept.

In reality politics often rests on the cultivation of fictions upon which narratives are constructed. The history of the modern Irish state is based on a series of political fictions. Within these political fictions politicians have wrestled with Ferdinand Tonnies's classic distinction between *Gemeinschaft* (community) and *Gesellschaft* (society). The first fiction of 'an Irish republic' was distinctly communitarian and traditional, and not in conformity with republican values as generally understood.

The Communitarian Republic and Militant Democracy

The nation-builders of the new Ireland sought to put the concept of 'local community' at the centre of their political vision. Paddy O'Carroll has observed in this regard:

> The small community was, therefore, not only the reality of the lives of most; it was also the key basis of their vision. As a cultural symbol central to most Irish identities of the time, community was an obvious rhetorical device to be used in the building of the nationalist state. It implied unity, wholeness and belonging; it imparted a strong sense of place and a hierarchy of entitlements. All of this reinforced in a commonsense way by Catholicism in general, by the experience of the Catholic parish locally and by the irrefragable unity of the image of the island.[37]

With the collapse of traditional community in Europe, Ireland fell back on a religious concept of the nation – based on traditional community. The idea was to find (or invent) a shared idea of national community, rather than social transformation. It was a collective political fiction contesting modernity that eschewed class politics in favour of a traditionalist vision of the past as the future. This was based on a morally centred ideal of community. The sustainable rural community came to embody the ideal of Ireland, spared from the pernicious influence of modern urban society. The parish became synonymous with the ideal of community. Priests became shamans of social Ireland totally dominating local civil society and exercising a hegemonic grip on the public sphere.

These kinds of cultural and political impulses have been characterised by Clifford Geertz as 'essentialism'.[38] He viewed them as characteristic of newly formed nation states. The vision of the 'community' as opposed to 'society' as a locus of the new nation state also evokes Tonnies's distinction between *Gemeinschaft* (community) and *Gesellschaft* (society).[39] Tonnies's social vision was shared by Ireland's nation-builders, most notably Eamon de Valera, arguably the nation's founding father. It was a traditionalist vision deeply rooted in cultural pessimism that feared modernity. Terence Brown observes that this pessimism was warranted, noting the 'spectacle of an Irish rural world without cultural hope or energy'.[40] Contemporaries shared this cultural pessimism. George Russell (Æ) (1867–1935) records, in his first journal the *Irish Statesman* (the voice of Fabianism in Ireland and alternate to the *New Statesman* in Britain), that in the immediate aftermath of independence there was social disintegration.

Faced with a series of challenges to the fledgling state, Eamon de Valera responded in a repressive manner to combat threats from militant republicans and the Blueshirts to Ireland's fragile democratic future. This strategy is called 'militant democracy', a term invented by Karl Loewenstein in 1937 to describe restrictions on civil and political freedom to contain fascism.[41] The most recent example of militant democracy was the withdrawal by several Irish universities of an invitation to speak to Nick Griffin MEP, leader of the

British National Party. Arguably, de Valera's version of militant democracy went further than the containment of republican and fascist threats. His 1937 constitution sought to reconcile popular sovereignty with Catholic social teaching, creating a conservative and distinctly sectarian state. The Irish constitution is not secular, since there is no separation between Church and state. It has resulted in major abuses of Catholic social power identified in the Ryan Report (2009), the Murphy Report (2009) and the Cloyne Report (2011) into clerical child abuse. But more fundamentally it circumscribed Irish democracy and repressed civil society – which was dominated throughout most of the twentieth century by the clergy.[42]

Modernisation, Sustainability and Political Fiction

The adoption of the project of modernisation from the 1960s onwards, involving entry into the European Community (now EU) in 1973, was to relocate Ireland's development trajectory within the global context, creating a new political fiction. It set the scene for the emergence of the Celtic Tiger economy, which became a metaphor for Ireland's reimagined development as a global urban society within the European Union. The debate about modernisation is essentially about models of development in this globalised context. As Ireland has moved from under-development through development to post-development – within the historical trajectory of the Irish state (founded in 1922) – new debates have emerged about the meaning and relevance of sustainability. The issue of the benefits of development, represented as 'good change' in public discourse, has been challenged by alternative models based on the goal of sustainable development. Following the emergence of the global economic crisis brought about by the collapse of international financial markets during 2008, new questions are being asked about the role of the state, as it seeks to deal with the consequences of market failure. Three models of development emerge in this modernisation debate, as illustrated in the table below.

Models of Development[43]

MODEL	IDEOLOGY	STRATEGY	GOAL	LOCATION
Market-led	Capitalism/ Neoliberalism	Modernisation	Globalisation	Economy
State-led	Social Democracy/ Marxism	State planning	Social equality	Politics/ Government
Community-led	Democracy/ Civic Republicanism	Citizen participation	Sustainable development	Civil society

The market-led model has been the dominant one in the age of globalisation, shaped by neoliberal ideology. But its hegemony has been challenged by the crash in 2008 and the requirement that the state save the market from total failure. The state-led model largely disappeared with the waning of socialism after 1989. The community-led model offers the only politically acceptable alternative to the market-led model in the contemporary world. This does not mean that the state-led model of development won't work. Up to the 1960s there was a concern in the West that the planned economy was more effective than the market-led model. Furthermore, the Chinese party-state model challenges the Western narrative of development based on the free market, representative democracy and the rule of law. The community-led model of development offers a new political fiction based on citizen participation and sustainability in a project that promises to rewrite the grammar of politics. It invites us to rethink the nature of modernity as an imaginary act. Cornelius Castoriadis in his book *The Imaginary Institution of Society* (1987) has argued that radical politics needs to move beyond the socialist (Marxist) exclusive preoccupation with capital. He redefines modernity as a struggle between the radical democratic project of autonomy (i.e. personal freedom to determine one's own future without structural manipulation) and the institutional project of mastery by the disciplinarian state. Writing about Castoriadis's theory, Gerald Delanty says that 'the focus on creativity offers an alternative theorisation of modernity echoing the idea of *homo faber* (man the maker) in Aristotle and Marx: the idea of society as an artefact created by human beings'.[44] New social movements within a reinvigorated civil society are playing a central role in reimagining political grammar in terms of being active citizens involved in a struggle for autonomy. Arguably, this is the progressive political fiction of postmodernity. This is a community-led model of development, based in civil society and inspired by the civic republican tradition of democracy that engages the citizenry in the polity, with the goal of sustainable development.

Sustainable communities provide a metaphor for deepening democratic politics that challenges previous ideologies of state or market dominance. It finds its most powerful expression in the New Bolivarianism that has reshaped the politics of Latin America – the first world region to disavow neoliberalism. But is it possible to reinvent Ireland's politics around the ideal of sustainable communities? Proposals from the Green Party in the last coalition government (2007–11) to devolve political decision-making to local communities suggests that the base of Irish democracy can be broadened. But in a global society we are left with the paradox of the placelessness of power and the powerlessness of place. This is the fundamental challenge that the idea of sustainable communities faces as a model of development, in a David and Goliath struggle for power.

Barack Obama in the *Audacity of Hope* (2008) built a presidential political platform around the generation of a new kind of politics. This is a politics that draws on the Ancient Greek tradition of civic republicanism, based on the ideal of sustainable democratic communities. In other words, the *agora*. President Obama has utilised his experience as a community organiser in Chicago to reinvigorate the concept of citizenship. His slogan 'yes, we can' invites the public to reimagine its relationship with the polity. The extraordinary political success of the Obama 2008 campaign was to create new political fiction at a time when Americans (and the rest of the world) were looking for change. President Obama, an advocate of reconciliation and participation, dreamt of a new Athens to replace the Sparta of the Bush administration – revitalised global democracy versus imperial military hegemony. This may be a Utopian vision that is at odds with *realpolitik* but it resonates with global progressive opinion. Political judgement will be passed on Obama's success or failure during 2012 in the presidential elections. His modest stimulus package, rescue of the banks and failure to reverse welfare reform have undermined the hope that the Obama presidency would be radical and transformational.

The Republic of Crisis: Apocalypse Now

Francis Ford Coppola's 1979 epic war film *Apocalypse Now* (an adaption of Joseph Conrad's novella *Heart of Darkness*) depicts modern war as a descent into primal madness. Set in the Vietnam War, it tells the story of war-weary Captain Willard (Martin Sheen) being dispatched to assassinate AWOL Renegade Colonel Kurtz (Marlon Brando) – secreted in the Cambodian jungle, where he is rumoured to have established himself as a local godhead. Kurtz's genocidal dictum 'Drop the Bomb: Exterminate them all', graphically illustrated by human heads mounted on stakes outside his compound, provides a hallucinatory Wagnerian quality to a film in which the insanity of the individual mirrors the insanity of the Vietnam War. The director struggled to find an ending to the film. This became a metaphor for the film itself in which reality and fantasy are merged. There is no purpose. Consequently, there can't be an end – at least not an end with a point, since futility on a grotesque scale has no point!

In a sense *Apocalypse Now* reflects the contemporary crisis that Ireland (arguably the most globalised country in the world) has inherited. It is hard to see an end to the crisis. Austerity (which makes recovery very difficult, if not impossible) is the officially supported policy in Dublin and Brussels. Yet, it doesn't seem to have a point – other than an ideological point. All of the escape routes have been closed off by the markets. The crisis has become political paralysis.

Slavoj Žižek argues in his book *Living at the End Times* (2011), that global capitalism is fast approaching its terminal crisis. He identifies the Four Horsemen of the Apocalypse as the worldwide ecological crisis; imbalances within the economic system; the biogenetic revolution; and exploding social divisions and ruptures. He characterises public reaction to this economic Armageddon in psychological terms as stages of grief: ideological denial, explosions of anger and attempts at bargaining, followed by depression and withdrawal.

Žižek's apocalyptic prediction of the end of global capitalism is not new. It is an end of civilisation thesis that has been around for half a century. It was propounded originally by Harvard professor Daniel Bell in his famous book *The End of Ideology* (1962) which claimed that the modernist project was exhausted and the acceptance of 'managed capitalism' was the only available political choice. The 'grand narratives' or 'big ideas' of the modern age were bankrupt. History was, after all, unchangeable. The future would be conservative. We have reached the ideological terminus of historical development, according to Bell. Similarly, Francis Fukuyama's book, *The End of History* (1992), claimed just that – the great ideological debates of the previous two centuries were over and liberal democracy in the form of market capitalism was triumphant. Socialism and transformative views of history were dead. Both Bell and Fukuyama and their many imitators in the millenarian preoccupation with 'endisms' were somewhat premature in their announcements. It is certainly true that the Western tradition of Enlightenment rationalism and belief in progress are in crisis. Whether this proves to be a terminal crisis remains to be seen. Both Bell and Fukuyama may be wrong in assuming that the future will be liberal and Western in the shape of American values. The Japanese philosopher Takeshi Umehara has observed that 'the total failure of Marxism . . . and the dramatic break up of the Soviet Union are only the precursors of the collapse of Western liberalism, the main current of modernity. Far from being the alternative to Marxism and the reigning ideology at the end of history, liberalism will be the next domino to fall.'[45] Islam laid down a dramatic challenge in the tragic events of 11 September 2001, when religious fanatics struck the heart of American economic and military power – the World Trade Center and the Pentagon. It has been followed by the erosion of civil liberties in the West that threatens the fabric of liberal democracy. This reflects a crisis of trust in democracy. Moreover, what we may be witnessing, as security increasingly dominates the agenda, is the end of politics as a forum for open debate, which is the crucible in which democracy flourishes. Tariq Ali comments from the vantage point of a lifelong political radical on the left of the spectrum:

> This closure of politics and economics produces fatal consequences. A disempowered people is constantly reminded of its own weakness. In the West a common response is to sink into the routines that dominate everyday life. Elsewhere in the world people become flustered, feel more and more helpless and nervous. Anger, frustration, despair multiply. They can no longer rely on the state to help. The laws favour the rich. So the more desperate amongst them, in search of a more meaningful existence or simply to break the monotony, begin to live by their own laws. Willing recruits will never be in short supply. The propaganda of the deed – the homage paid by the weak to the strong – will endure. It is the response of atomised individuals to a world that no longer listens, to politicians who have become interchangeable, to the corporations one-eyed in the search for profits and global media networks owned by the self-same corporations and locked into a relationship of mutual dependence with the politicians. This is the existential misery that breeds

insecurity and fosters deadly hatreds. If the damage is not repaired, sporadic outbursts of violence will continue to intensify.[46]

Ali's point is that Islamic terrorists in their 9/11 attack on the World Trade Center were asserting the primacy of religion over trade – God over capital and ultimately Islam over the Western tradition of modernity.

Ireland is at the epicentre of this global crisis. While we successfully ended the terrorist war in Northern Ireland through the 1998 Belfast Agreement, economic hubris has created a new crisis of unparalleled proportions. During our enthralment to the imaginary Celtic Tiger, arguably we became self-absorbed subjects (consumer citizens) rather than active citizens engaged in society. It was a perfect fantasy land – beyond the reach of reality, in which we borrowed from the future in a wager that we lost.

In post-Celtic Tiger Ireland, we are experiencing what Žižek calls the '*real* real', which he likens to the horror in a horror film. The line between politics and fantasy has become blurred in our contemporary reality. This presents Irish citizens with a series of questions:

- How can we overcome being subjects?
- How do we restore content to our republican imaginary?
- How do we deal with the destruction of the Celtic Tiger inheritance?

The answers must be based on an attempt to reclaim political reality. First, we must discover the difference between truth and falsehood. Second, we are challenged to explore new republican models and narratives in search of answers. Third, we need to reinvent politics in the form of a critical citizenship based on inclusion and participation, in which the self and others interact in a new narrative of the republic. Finally, we need to rediscover society in the form of sustainable communities, populated by *real* people.

How can this be done? The new Irish President, poet and intellectual Michael D. Higgins, in his book *Renewing the Republic* has set out an agenda:

> I believe we must now promote a positive vision of what it means to be a citizen in Ireland. This citizenship should be based on equality and respect, with a basic level of rights and participation – a citizenship floor – below which no one should be allowed to fall. We need to move away from radical individualisation towards a radical kind of inclusion.
>
> Inclusion means valuing diversity in all its forms and challenging exclusion wherever it occurs. No one in our society should experience the destructive effects of discrimination, isolation or rejection.
>
> Inclusion means celebrating solidarity by recognising the aspirations, concerns, creativity and potential of every citizen, regardless of the age, orientation, capacities or means. Inclusive citizenship also brings shared responsibility – a life that goes beyond the self to include those around us and, indeed, the generations yet to come.[47]

The Irish President advocates a creative society constructed from the bottom up:

The creative society cannot be imposed from above;
it is built on creativity made possible by sustainable
communities. Properly respected, the cultural space can
be an invitation to push the boundaries of the possible –
enfranchising us all in our capacity for living, and
enriching the social and economic life of the nation.[48]

He argues that the alternative is Žižek's Apocalypse:

Should the adjustment in economic and social assumptions prove to be incapable of being made, we probably
face an unmediated confrontation between the excluded
and those who chose to be unconcerned. Such a point is
the one at which the dark prescriptions of Slavoj Žižek
become relevant. Around the world there is evidence
that such an outcome is achieving momentum, and some
support.[49]

President Higgins concludes with his own apocalyptic warning:

We are drifting to a final rupture between the economy,
politics and society. If it happens, the ensuing conflict will
not be mediated through trade unions, political parties
or social movements. It will be a naked confrontation
between, on the one side, the wealthy getting wealthier,
and the poor getting poorer; between the excluded and
the powerful; between the technologically manipulated.
It will be a conflict as raw as any in history of private
accumulation between, on the one hand, consumers, and,
on the other, the excluded poor, who no longer have any
norms of citizenship that they share or which would
mediate their conflict.

Public participation is now falling in every institution of civil society. The norms of a shared life have little opportunity of being articulated. That is the inescapable other side of the coin of globalisation, which is the unaccountable economy on a world scale. That is why it is necessary for the Left to outline the case for a new and vibrant citizenship that can vindicate such values as solidarity, community, democracy, justice, freedom and equality. These values can be achieved by giving them a practical expression in a new theory of citizenship.[50]

The challenge that President Higgins has presented is essentially about the need for a new political fiction to take the narrative of the Irish Republic forward. It is very clearly framed within the language of civil society: community, inclusive citizenship and sustainability.

Arguably, President Higgins's vision of a political rupture generated by bottom-up forces within civil society points to the social left, as opposed to the political left, as the drivers of change in post-politics society. The Occupy movement (now experiencing suppression in New York, London and Dublin) is the most visible contemporary manifestation of the social left as an actor in post-politics. In response to the eviction of the protestors from the grounds of St Paul's Cathedral the *Guardian* (29 February 2012) declared on its front page:

You cannot evict an idea. Such is the message of defiance from Occupy. But it is not entirely true. For the whole point of Occupy is that it's not just an idea bouncing around the internet. Occupy is stubbornly about the physical reality of space. Others may write books and organise seminars. Occupy puts up tents. It takes up space. It is there.

Sarah van Gelder likens the Occupy movement to the Arab spring and argues that its name identifies the cause of the current crisis: 'Wall street banks, big corporations, and others among the 1% are claiming the world's wealth for themselves at the expense of the 99% and having their way with governments.'[51] What is refreshing about the Occupy movements is their determination to link their political critique of capitalism to practical welfare initiatives aimed at the socially excluded. Despite their chaos they genuinely represent a search for truth.

President Higgins's concept of a 'creative society' has been taken up by the Cork Occupy movement as a philosophical basis of its protest:

A hugely important aspect of the protest was the involvement of Cork Community Art Link, who brought a real creative and artistic colour to the demonstration. This combines the importance of our presence on the South Mall in the heart of the city with an appreciation of the need to move in more creative directions, opening up the Occupy movement to all. This is about making the movement accessible and welcoming to all, and bringing that together with the principles of equality and democracy that are central to what we do. In a time where there is such an overwhelming amount and range of advertising constantly being forced down our throats, we need to work in ways that really engage with people, and the wide and open nature of the Occupy movement is bringing something really new to the table.

Creative protests such as the Parade are testament to a DIY ethic producing our own culture, one that can be defiant through creativity, but this shouldn't be seen as the be-all and end-all of how we're to organise ourselves for this fight. We should not feel bound to the past to feel we owe today's struggle to those who've come before us – we should try to see ourselves within the tradition of human beings standing up for potent ideas of justice, equality and dignity. How we interpret that challenge of building a new society should be across the whole spectrum of human capacity – the creative and cultural shouldn't be seen as opposed to the political, to the practical task of organising and mobilising in cooperation with one another, against those whose interests are currently served by our rights being stamped on.[52]

The Occupy movement is part of a new political fiction that is creating a participative democratic narrative in which citizens are becoming actors in making their own history. It suggests that we are experiencing 'the democratisation of democracy' in response to the invisibility of autocratic power that seeks to mould contemporary political reality – and fails.

A 'Second Republic': A New Political Fiction?

A new political fiction requires a new grammar that is both emancipatory and republican. The challenge for the community-led model is to forge a new social and cultural grammar, which can deepen democracy. That involves confronting global hegemonic forces 'by the initiatives of grassroots organisations, of local and popular movements that endeavour to counteract extreme forms of social exclusion and open up new spaces for democratic participation'.[53] It also involves addressing Weber's 'iron cage of bureaucracy', which undermines democratic practice by subordinating the citizen to the bureaucratic state apparatus.[54] In turn that involves challenging the hegemonic conception of representative democracy (thin) by participatory democracy (thick) in a new synthesis that realigns politics to civil society in a project of demodiversity, based on greater citizen engagement in politics.[55] To put it concisely, the idea of sustainable community is the late-modern *agora,* where the citizen can democratically challenge oligarchies of wealth (capitalism) and power (bureaucratic state).

Peadar Kirby and Mary P. Murphy in their book *Towards a Second Republic* (2011) have proposed a complete restructuring of Irish institutions, economy and society. It presupposes that there was a 'First Republic', which Fintan O'Toole, citing Samuel Beckett, suggests may be a farcical idea, albeit one rooted in the Marxist Democratic Programme (1919).[56] It was of course the stillborn child of the Irish Revolution. The Second Republic movement has argued the case for a citizens' assembly. The Fine Gael–Labour government, elected in 2011, promised a 'democratic revolution'. A constitutional convention was presented as the means to achieve this goal. While the aspiration of the government to reimagine Irish politics is very impressive, so far plans have been more limited. Abolishing the Seanad is a controversial proposal since it arguably will constrain democracy. Limiting the tenure of the President from seven to five years is another proposal that is being considered. More radically the government has indicated its willingness to lower the voting age – empowering young people. This is welcome and progressive. But the real test of the proposed constitutional convention will be in its composition (what will be the level of citizen participation?), process (will citizens be empowered to set the agenda?), outcome (contractarian, i.e. pro-business, or solidaristic, i.e. pro-society?) and the status of its recommendations (will it be consultative or binding?). Finally, if it is to produce a republican constitution there must be separation between Church and state. Otherwise, there will be no 'Second Republic' as there was no 'First Republic'!

Linda Connolly and Niamh Hourigan have demonstrated the capacity of Irish social movements to bring about transformative change.[57] Arguably, change will not come through the political-party system, which is still constrained by the historical over-hang of militant democracy that has limited public debate. Trust is more likely to be embedded in civil society. But, as Peadar Kirby and Mary P. Murphy demonstrate, Irish civil society is very diverse: ranging from neoliberal (wedded to traditional voluntarism, building social capital and restoration of economic competitiveness); through social democratic perspectives driven by the values of equality and solidarity; to environmental orientations (concerned with sustainability, planetary citizenship and ecological justice).[58] It is possible that some civil-society actors could coalesce around the concept of a social left, based on a shared vision of critical citizenship founded on the principles of social inclusion and democratic participation, as a republican strategy. If we are to imagine a Second Republic in which the population genuinely feel like citizens as opposed to subjects, then there will need to be a core set of principles. Ten principles for critical citizenship are set out below:

Ten Principles for Critical Citizenship

1 Campaign for social justice – reject growing inequality:
   a Inequality causes poverty
   b Inequality causes social conflict
   c Inequality ruins lives
   d Inequality is a product of a market society
   e Inequality is based on oligarchy and is the antithesis of democracy.
2 Seek to 'democratise democracy' though public accountability, e.g. the banks, the political class, multiple ownership of property, links between politics and business, clientalism, etc.
3 Challenge monopoly of knowledge in information society – 'another world is possible'.
4 Demand the state upholds the planning laws, based on the principles of proper planning and sustainable development.
5 Broaden the political debate beyond a preoccupation with narrow economic concerns to social justice and sustainable community development. We can survive the crash by reinventing solidarity.
6 The creation of participatory democratic spaces at grass-roots community level that values the citizens' 'lived experience'.
7 Social action provides information and empowerment which empowers the citizen to know and understand what is going on in an increasingly changing society, based on cyber democracy – 'Think Global, Act Local'.
8 Build 'poor peoples'' social movements that challenge political parties' monopoly of power.

9 Promote 'Rights Talk' as the basis of critical citizenship
  – why should anybody be poor?
10 Build a strong democracy in Ireland based on 'thick'
   participation rather than 'thin' representation – reinvent
   Irish democracy.

'Up the Republic' now has the ring of a funeral dirge for a
dead political project. The undertakers are here in the form of
the troika (EU, ECB, IMF). They are grave, respectful and
even understanding of our misery – as good undertakers
should be! The grief reaction among the citizens for their lost
sovereignty varies from denial through anger to despairing
acceptance. There is a rupture with the past, but with no clear
vision of the future that isn't apocalyptic. In the circumstances, the president has gently reminded the citizens that
they have the power to construct their own future. His democratic vision is for a bottom-up renewal. He wants us to forge
our own political fiction, in which we once again become
actors in making our own history. We are invited by the president to deepen our democracy, think for ourselves, and shape
our own destiny. Oddly, this sounds strangely counter-
intuitive. Like Benjamin Barber's caged animals, we don't like
to leave the comfort of the cage even though the President has
opened its door. Somehow, we remain mesmerised like the
characters in Haruki Murakami's novel *IQ84*. But there are
voices of protest. The Occupy movement has attracted public support because its members dared to step outside their
personal cages and enter the public sphere. But of course we
are told that it is private space and they must be moved on.
They are making democratic noises, which the authorities
judge to be an unreasonable provocation of the citizens. Despite their public support, their protest is being suppressed.

The Occupy movement resembles those campaigns for the right of association that gave birth to democracy during the eighteenth and nineteenth centuries. That resulted in the twentieth-century welfare state, the good society that benefited citizens. It too is being suppressed, however successful and compatible with a burgeoning economy. Social justice is a forbidden language in the twenty-first century. Our gentle undertakers – those global civil servants – point towards the cages, where the living dead are to be consigned. Up the Second Republic!

7

Republican Reflections on the Occupy Movements[1]

PHILIP PETTIT

What do you say to thousands of young people who gather in frustration at a political system that has utterly failed them? Is there anything to say that can reach the depth of their wholly understandable outrage at the disappearance of jobs and the collapse of prospects?

As someone associated in an unusual way with the 2004–11 government of Spanish Prime Minister José Luis Zapatero, I cannot avoid that question. Asked to report on the performance of that administration in the 2004–8 parliament, in particular its fidelity to the republican principles I espouse, I gave it a high mark. So what do I say four years later?

In thinking about the future of Spain under the Zapatero government – indeed under any government – I made two serious mistakes. I was naive about the reliability of the international financial system in providing the infrastructure that would enable the government in a country such as Spain to provide for its people's economic welfare. And I failed to realise how far the country's options for responding to a downturn of economic fortunes would be restricted by its membership of the eurozone.

I continue to commend the performance of the Zapatero government for its attempts to equalise the position of women in society, for its regularisation of the status of many illegal immigrants, for the law of dependency that it established in protection of the vulnerable, and for the introduction of same-sex marriage. And I still commend it for the independence that it gave to the national broadcaster, for the greater degree of transparency that it brought to government business and for establishing Spain in the role of a model international citizen.

All of these initiatives were important steps towards the realisation of what I see as republican goals. The republican ideal is that of living in freedom, without being subject to the dominating will of an individual or body that is capable of interfering without licence in your central life choices. As an ideal of justice, it holds out the prospect of a society in which people are resourced and protected against private domination in the enjoyment of such choices. As an ideal of democracy, it offers the promise of a regime in which the government that has responsibility for justice is not itself publicly dominating, being forced to operate on accepted, popular terms. And as an ideal of international relations, it directs us to the prospect of a world in which no peoples are dominated by other peoples or by multinational or international bodies.

Many of the Zapatero initiatives were explicitly designed to advance such goals and are signal, hopefully lasting, achievements. But now is not the time for praise. Now is a time for taking stock and thinking about where we go from here. So what are the lessons that have been taught by the painful experiences of the last three or four years? In particular, what are the lessons for those who espouse broadly republican ideals? I concentrate on lessons for the relationship between government and the economy, though I recognise, as I mention in the conclusion, that there may be wider and deeper lessons to be learned as well.

Riding the Tiger

The crisis showed us all that the reliance of governments on the international financial system amounts, in an old phrase, to riding the tiger. All governments depend on the bond market for financing national projects, especially within a fixed currency area such as the eurozone; this is no more surprising than the fact that homeowners rely on mortgage providers for purchasing their apartments or houses. And all governments depend on the banking system and stock market, of course, for the capital that nurtures job-creating enterprises. This dependence makes for a serious vulnerability to the performance of the international financial system.

The system on which our governments depend – in my image, the tiger that they ride – is often presented as a body of individuals with a concerted will of their own: a cadre of international financiers and bankers that acts with a single, self-aggrandising aim. It would be nice if things were like that, for such an entity would then offer a lightning rod for our outrage, a target for our resentment, an agency that we might expect to be able to censure and hold to account. But alas, as always, things are more complicated.

The tiger that our governments ride is a more wayward and untameable beast than the body imagined in such a conspiracy theory. Its movements are dictated by motives no less self-seeking and callous than those projected in that theory. But they are dictated from a thousand or more sources, making the performance of the tiger an unpredictable precipitate of multiple inputs. The behaviour of this tiger is as directionless and thoughtless, and often as turbulent, as the shifts of wind in a storm.

A number of countries, particularly in Europe, are now exposed to the worst of those winds. An imported financial crisis has led to unemployment; unemployment payments to an increased government deficit; the rise in that deficit to bond-market uncertainty; and this uncertainty to increased borrowing costs. The fear of a further increase in costs has inhibited the potential of the government to respond to unemployment by Keynesian, pump-priming methods of economic stimulation, since they require budget deficits. And the constraints of the eurozone have made it close to impossible for the government to manage the crisis by devaluing the currency or defaulting on its debt. We are in the midst of a perfect storm.

How should European countries respond to this experience? How, more generally, should the peoples of the world respond? Do we have the capacity to assert ourselves democratically against the tiger of the financial system? Or are we forever subject to the whims and moods of a capricious beast?

Two Radical Responses

There are two extreme responses that the financial crisis and its aftermath have provoked. One is to say that all will be well if our governments stop trying to anticipate and deflect the movements of the tiger by propping up and bailing out the bodies that they judge too big to fail. This approach, exemplified in the stance of the Tea Party in the United States, amounts to pre-emptive surrender in face of the profit-seeking ventures of credit and capital. It gives government the task of law and order and calls for the abdication of the state in the sphere of production, commerce and employment.

This first response would downsize and marginalise government, letting the market rule unimpeded in the financial and material economy. The second radical response would recommend the very opposite. It would support a rejection of dependence on the sort of beast that the international financial system constitutes. Where the first approach would give the tiger free range, this would simply kill the animal. Those attracted to the response complain that so long as the tiger survives, we all live at its mercy. They recommend that we should reject dependency on impersonal market forces and reclaim our status as a democratic people, our standing as rulers of our individual and collective lives.

Because they are simple, these two responses have a natural attraction at a time of extreme crisis. It is comforting to think that all will be well if we can only liberate the power of the market or if we can only reassert our will as a people. But because the responses are simplistic, we should back away from both.

The Mistakes in These Responses

The first response puts its faith in the invisible hand of market-based adjustments, oblivious to the fact that it is governments who fix the laws under which titles of ownership are established, rights of property and trade are determined, the money supply is controlled, and the very capacity for incorporation that is exercised in the formation of banks and companies is defined. There is little plausibility or attraction in the ideal it hails. It would license a plutocratic regime in which markets allow enormous concentrations of personal and corporate wealth and the polity does nothing about restraining the power of those thereby enriched.

The second approach puts its faith in a more attractive object than the first, appealing to the sense of our collective power as a democratic people; it is populist in character rather than plutocratic. But this approach is equally blind to blatant fact. It suggests that we can rely on democratic decision-making to call an economic and financial system into being, relying on centralised planning or co-ordination, all on its own, to establish a viable system of credit and a functional market. And that is wholly implausible.

The creation of an economic and financial system requires a people and a government to recruit private sources of wealth and investment in the enterprise of building a prosperous society. And this means building with what Kant called the crooked timber of humanity. It requires acknowledging the imperfect motives and the limiting constraints of people's psychology and sociology and devising institutions that can survive in the presence of such more or less fixed parameters. Even the most democratically inspired institutions will fail unless they are able to take root in the human environment that these parameters define.

This human environment relates to democratic progress in the building of viable institutions much as the natural environment relates material progress in the technological use of the earth. The natural environment offers us rich resources of nutrition and energy but these resources are scarce and, as we now know to our cost, extremely hard to sustain. In parallel, the human environment promises us rich prospects of production, trade and employment but access to these prospects is also problematic. Their availability depends on how much confidence individuals and groups can be brought to invest in one another and on how much credit they can be persuaded to extend.

As a species, we have done many things surprisingly well in building a society that copes with the limitations of natural and human environments. The technologies accumulated in agriculture and industry have transformed the natural environment and bent it to our human will, enabling us to do more than scratch a bare living from the soil. And the ideals and institutions elaborated in our political and democratic practice hold out at least the possibility of a human environment in which we can claim shared responsibility for collective arrangements and can enjoy equal respect under those arrangements. This is the ideal of a democratic republic in which we can each walk tall, conscious of being sufficiently resourced and protected to be able to make our own way in the world – conscious, in effect, of enjoying a freedom that gives us independence from the will or domination of any individual or group.

If we are to do well on the technological front, achieving material progress, then we must clearly work within the limitations of the natural or physical environment. And if we are to do well on the institutional front, achieving democratic progress, then we must work equally within the constraints imposed by the psychological and sociological realities of human life. Long tradition teaches us about those realities. It counsels us that power corrupts, for example, and that those we empower should always be held accountable. It teaches us that no one is proof against temptation, so that no one should be given unconstrained opportunity for self-enrichment. And it teaches us that everybody's business is nobody's business and that in general, as Aristotle observes, people will look after their own property better than they will look after what belongs to all. We ignore these constraints at our peril when we offer proposals for democratic, institutional design.

The populist fallacy is precisely that of ignoring constraints of this kind and imagining that we can construct the great society without heed to the recalcitrance of the human material, the crookedness of the human timber, with which we build. It may not be as salient a fallacy as the plutocratic counterpart but it is just as dangerous. Thus it would encourage us to be complacent about the possibility of building a system of confidence and credit, which any flourishing democracy requires, without having to worry about its compatibility with the often uncongenial instincts and limitations of our human make-up. It would foster the illusion that there is a new, secular Jerusalem within our immediate, collective reach: that all it requires to get there is good will.

The Lesson of the Financial Crisis and its Aftermath

The looming shortage of fossil fuels, the manifest danger of relying on nuclear energy and the threat of climate change have made us all aware of how fragile are the technologies whereby we maintain synergy with our natural environment. And the financial crisis, I would say, teaches a parallel lesson in the human domain. It has shown us how fragile are the institutions whereby we promote successful government and preserve democratic control over our lives. In particular, it has demonstrated the ease with which institutional changes in the organisation of banking – the deregulation pursued with reckless abandon over the ten years preceding the crisis – can jeopardise the existence of the confidence and credit on which our democracies rely for the economic welfare of their citizens.

The deregulation that was introduced prior to the financial crisis was prompted by a disastrous indifference, on a par with the populist indifference just described, to the Kantian counsel of recognising that the timber of humanity is crooked. Consider the developments whereby those in the financial sector were allowed to blur the lines between high street and investment banking, to lend and invest on the basis of an ever smaller asset base, to divide and package debt obligations so that risk became utterly opaque, to allow for unsustainable levels of insurance against default, and to perpetrate a popular illusion that the temporary growth thereby stimulated was based on solid economic achievement. Whether or not these developments were promoted by the financial sector on a good-faith basis, they created a milieu in which the desire for quick, often fabulous, profits generated a frenzy of risk-taking and visited a tragedy on people worldwide.

None of us can contemplate with analytical detachment the ravages that the self-seeking few, operating within the newly deregulated environment, imposed on the rest of humanity. None can contemplate those ravages without moral indignation at the fact that only a tiny percentage of those few have had to pay a legal or even an economic price for their activity. And none can contemplate the ravages without extreme outrage at the realisation that most of the few have gone on to thrive and prosper, even as the many have had to face unemployment, austerity and downright poverty. The thing beggars belief.

But while the performance of financial operatives may beggar belief, on reflection it ought not to be very surprising. Over two thousand years ago Plato invoked the ring of Gyges to suggest that few of us would prove virtuous, were we able to wear a ring that gave us invisibility and impunity in the pursuit of our own pleasures. It is a sad fact of human nature that while many of us might not be corrupt, not many are incorruptible; when opportunity offers not many are capable of resisting the temptation to make a quick buck. The timber may not be rotten but it is crooked. Given the amazing opportunities that individuals and organisations in the financial sector enjoyed under the new deregulation, it should probably not shock us that those opportunities were exploited to maximum advantage.

Beyond Plutocracy and Populism

How then should we respond to the financial crisis and its aftermath? We should certainly avoid the iconoclastic urge to seek the demolition of either the governmental or the financial system. There is no case for advocating the abdication of democratic responsibility in the manner of the plutocratic response or for denying the need to ride the tiger of an independent financial system in the manner of the populist. The tiger is not to be given free range and the tiger is not to be hunted down and killed.

The response required, in a third alternative that our metaphor suggests, is to rein in and regulate the tiger: to put it to work for democratic ends, under restrictions that make sure it serves those ends. The challenge is to devise a regulative regime in which the financial system can continue to provide us with resources of credit without giving financial insiders the opportunity or incentive for activities that endanger the overall, common good.

This is a democratic and not just a technocratic challenge. It will certainly require technical expertise to identify means whereby a financial system that has novel instruments at its disposal can still be regulated and harnessed to the common good. But it is up to a responsible parliament and a contestatory citizenry to explore the strengths and weaknesses of different proposals and to maintain oversight of whatever proposal is eventually enacted.

How can a contestatory citizenry function in a role of this kind? The Italian-Atlantic tradition of republicanism suggests that if citizens are to exercise the contestatory control that democracy requires, then they must divide the civic labour of contestation between them, with different groups specialising in different areas of governmental activity; here as in other areas power must be dispersed. Contemporary society is too complex to enable the virtuous citizen, or even the body of virtuous citizens as a whole, to interrogate government on every front. It is essential for the proper invigilation of those in power that different civic associations can monitor the decisions of the authorities in different areas of policy-making, can muster the best available expertise in assessing what the authorities decide, and can hold them to effective, public account.

The 15-M movement in Spain, and the Occupy movements in other countries, have been important in giving expression to the insistence of the people at large that government should live up to their expectations on the economic and related fronts. But if it is to have a lasting impact on how government is pursued, then it must generate more specialised associations for the interrogation of government policy. Democracy is hard, often boring, work and it is vital that the democratic energy behind these movements is channelled in such directions. Otherwise it is likely to be as evanescent in its impact as a New Year's Eve fireworks display.

But while the challenge identified is democratic rather than just technocratic in character, it engages democracy on the international as well as the national front. The financial crisis began in the United States and spread elsewhere via the exposure of financial houses in other countries to the complex and opaque risks manufactured in America. Moreover, the austerity programme imposed in the aftermath of the financial crisis is the artefact of a skittish, international bond market and a determination on the part of a range of countries, particularly those in the European Union, to assure the market that neither they nor the countries they bail out of trouble will resort to pump-priming methods of economic stimulation.

The international nature of the challenge, like the technocratic, does not mean that it is not truly democratic in character. But it does mean that if people are to address it seriously in the contestatory mode I envisage, then they have to do so via civic associations that reach across boundaries. Fully alerting governments to the urgency of popular demand might be better achieved by marches across Europe than by mass gatherings in national squares. And the dubious case for pan-European austerity might be most effectively interrogated and tested by the trans-national, non-governmental organisations that such marches would support.

None of us who applauded the performance of government – any government – in the years prior to the financial crisis can be complacent about what has transpired since then in countries such as Spain, let alone countries such as Greece and Portugal and my own native Ireland. The experience of these countries is humiliating for any commentator who celebrated government success. We thought and said that things were going well but all the time there was a perfect storm in the making.

Apology aside, however, there are three points emerging from the previous discussion that I would like to emphasise. First, the achievements of the Zapatero government in those years should not be overlooked; they remain important and, I hope, lasting. Second, the failure of the government to provide for the employment prospects of its people should not prompt us to lurch into either of the iconoclastic positions I described; it should alert us to the importance of governmental regulation over the financial system and of democratic invigilation of the regulatory regime established. And third, the democratic challenge to government in the area of financial regulation and economic policy should be taken to the European level, not just left at the national; the civic associations on which it depends must assume a cross-country, EU-wide profile.

This essay has concentrated on the failure of government on the financial and economic front, since the stimulus to the 15-M and the Occupy movements has been the collapse in the jobs market. But the challenges that civic associations can make on government in furtherance of important goals are not limited, of course, to the financial front. The complaints generated by the movement run much deeper, casting doubt on the character of existing democratic parties, for example, and on their claim to be able to give voice to popular demand. But here too, if the movement is to make a permanent impact on public life, it has to get serious about issues of institutional design. It has to be able to generate proposals for change and it has to be able to command a hearing for those proposals in the popular press and within the political parties, in the parliament and at the polls. I trust that it will be able to generate discussion and open up decision on these wide-ranging matters. To the extent that it succeeds, democracy will be the winner: democracy in Spain and, by example, democracy in other countries too.

8

Law, Poetry and the Republic

THEO DORGAN

It is a fundamental duty of the state to manage the economy in order to provide for the common good. In so far as we are self-constituted as a republic, that duty is a solemn obligation conferred by the citizens acting in concert as citizens of the republic. The state, considered as the apparatus of governance in its entirety, derives its authority and legitimacy from the citizens who in their totality as free men and women constitute the republic; the right of the state to discharge the duties and obligations of a sovereign government is no more and no less than the devolved right to exercise the prior sovereignty of the republic.

It follows that the ceding of economic sovereignty is also an undermining of the sovereignty of the republic. The state, in so far as it takes its instructions from an external power, can no longer claim co-identification with the republic, an instrumental fiction that has proved useful up to now. In the most absolute sense possible, the continuing existence of the republic as a sovereign entity has been called into question.

What is to be done with our poor battered republic is not just an open question; it is a question that keeps on opening out into further questions, so much so that one begins to wonder if we'll ever find a way to get started on the process of rebuilding.

It seems to me we are still at the diagnostic stage, still trying to get a grip on the extent and nature of what is wrong before we can formulate even tentative proposals as to what is to be done. It may even be that rebuilding will prove impossible, in which case we shall find ourselves looking at a profound rupture, at the refounding rather than the reformulation of the republic and hence the state.

It is still an open question whether rebuilding is even possible; it may well prove to be, when all the analysis is complete, that we need to start over again from an entirely new set of assumptions as to what kind of state is needed to provide for the republic, for the common good in the twenty-first century.

One thing we can say for certain: piecemeal reform of an ad hoc kind is likely to leave intact what we might call the armature or infrastructure of the state, its accumulated burden of law, language and custom.

The state apparatus derives its ultimate authority from that regular consultation with the will of the people that we are pleased to call the representative democratic process. In theory, it works like this: we the people choose representatives freely, and those representatives, acting on our behalf, choose a government. Our primary influence on who forms that government is fatally circumscribed, in most instances, by a kind of a priori sleight of hand: strictly speaking, we cast our votes to select an individual as our representative, but in all likelihood that representative will have a prior allegiance to a party and a policy, and should that party enter into government, our representative will almost invariably find herself or himself disposed if not actually constrained to put party allegiance before the expressed interests of those people who elected her or him. No longer able (or perhaps willing) to act as a direct representative of his or her constituency's wishes, the individual deputy finds himself or herself co-opted by the unquestioned supposition that in voting for that individual we are, in effect, giving a free hand to his or her party to pursue its policy goals. Even when there are grounds to believe that the people *in toto* do not approve of a particular policy, the party in government will claim that it has a free hand until the next election, and that the individual deputy must in effect surrender his or her direct responsibility to a particular cohort of electors in favour of the party's will.

Once it enters into office according to law, the government assumes, crucially, responsibility for ensuring the continued operation of that corpus of laws it inherits, and it acquires the power both to amend existing laws and to promulgate further laws.

In effect, the government enters into possession of the law, and into ownership of the language of law. This further fuels the inexorable alienation of the government from the people.

If party allegiance is the first dilution of the contract between we the people on the one hand and the aggregate of our chosen representatives on the other, then the second dilution comes from a profound misunderstanding. Naively, a majority of the people believe, might always have believed, that there is a necessary connection between law and justice understood as fairness; that the state is concerned with delivering justice by means of policy and the law.

Neither the possessors nor the enforcers of law are under this illusion.

Bertrand Russell was of the opinion that: 'Law in origin was merely a codification of the power of dominant groups, and did not aim at anything that to a modern man would appear to be justice.' The late and unlamented J. Edgar Hoover believed that: 'Justice is incidental to law and order.'

When the citizen looks at the law, even when she hopes to benefit from it, she is always looking upward, towards the apex of a pyramid of power, towards that small handful of people who, in effect, own the law.

This is the dynamic underpinning the well-known anarchist slogans: 'Don't vote, it only encourages them', and 'No matter who you vote for, the government always gets in.'

Who makes the law? The naive believe that government makes the law, and instrumentally, though to a very limited extent, this is true. It is more useful, and in a broader sense more true, to say that the state makes the law, and we should always bear in mind that the incumbent government is no more than a part of, perhaps not always the most powerful component of, the state.

What is a law? Let us agree to speak of it for the moment as a directive arising from desire, embodied in language.

That desire, which is in essence a desire of governance, is a desire of the state.

The state desires that we refrain from murdering one another, for instance. In order to inhibit murder, the state frames a set of prohibitions in language, and a consequent set of punishments for transgressors of those prohibitions. These prohibitions make the transition from desire to instrument once they are embodied in language.

The state might equally wish explicitly to permit some action or other, and from time to time, when it is considered desirable for one reason or another, the state will frame a law that permits some action, or calls something into being. These permissions, too, will appear in the world framed in language, framed as a particular kind of text.

These texts, these directives, we call laws. We are accustomed to thinking of laws as relatively simple exercises in language. A law says, for instance: You may do this or, you may not do this other . . . I am not at all sure that this process is anything like as clear-cut and straightforward as it seems. In fact, these instruments in language are complex phenomena.

Firstly, in order to promulgate this law, the state must have the authority to do so. In our small republic, setting aside the historical processes that brought the state into existence, this authority derives from the constitution. It is by virtue of authority deriving from the constitution that the state is empowered to speak to us in the laws.

To be sure, laws are framed by the government of the day, which derives its immediate authority to make and enforce laws from the democratic election process, but the validating matrix of any given law is the constitution.

Thus, the first test of whether or not a law is a true law is its constitutionality; that is, the concepts and meanings that can be said legitimately to inhere in the law must be put through a linguistic process that tests whether or not there is agreement between the language of the law and the language of the constitution.

A law, then, is framed in a particular voice; the law speaks to us *de haut en bas*. Law must be founded on authority, and the language of lawgiving necessarily derives from precedent, by which I mean here linguistic precedent.

A law, to put it simply, cannot employ arbitrary language. Moreover, it would be rare indeed if a law could be success-fully framed in colloquial language – imagine, if you will, a law against murder that said, simply, 'Ah here, you can't be going around killing people.'

The framers of laws are hedged around by inherited prohibitions, constrained by linguistic precedent, limited to a specific instrumental vocabulary, syntax and grammar.

Here is a major source of the unease most people feel in the face of the law. On the one hand, the state derives its authority under the constitution from the people. Without their consent to be governed, the people owe no allegiance to the state, nor can the state presume to frame laws and expect them to have and take effect. The constitution itself, which stands behind the state in its framing of laws, derives *its* authority from the people, too. The constitution, put to us as a proposal framed and expressed in words, takes effect with our assent as authority in language. Yet the language of law, as the language of the constitution, might as well exist in a different universe as far as the daily language of the people is concerned. The linguist Ferdinand de Saussure distinguished between two aspects of the use of language, aspects to which he gave the terms '*langue*' and '*parole*'. '*Langue*', to put it very simply, is official language, bourgeois and conservative language if you like. '*Parole*' is the common speech of everyday life.

Law is always and everywhere '*langue*'. It aspires to the qualities of fixedness: of fixed definitions, custom-enshrined usage, precedent, singularity of meaning. Law, if I might put it like this, aspires to a kind of marmoreal perfection; it aspires to the condition of language carved in stone.

'*Parole*', on the other hand, is flux and swerve, a busyness of constant renewal, a thing of tones and shades of meaning, inventive, protean, multilayered, a hare jinking through a field as opposed to a horse dreaming of its apotheosis in bronze.

All societies ruled by law will continue to accumulate laws in the light of Zeno's paradox, always approaching by smaller and smaller increments towards that unreachable state of perfection where everything that can be permitted has been defined and provided for, everything to be forbidden has been accounted for.

Laws, taken in their accumulation through time, tend towards a world view where life can be framed and conducted in the light of fixities and definites – which is so much at variance with life as we actually experience it that there is and must be a constant necessary tension between life and law.

Law, as I am framing it here, is hieratic, and every *hieros* must have its servants and hierophants – in this case its enforcers and explainers.

Because law in our time has the status of constituted mystery, as religion once had, in many places still has, the language of law has become a reserved language, and must therefore have its interpreters if it is to be made intelligible to us the people. These interpreters, seen horizontally, evaluate one another in accordance with each individual's skill at interpreting, parsing and deploying the language of the law. Because of the intrinsic stasis or tendency towards stasis of the whole system, there is also a vertical distribution of adepts, with the implicit assumption that those most versed in the law will occupy positions closest to the apex of the mystery, and that conversely those entering into the service of the law will do so at a level where the appropriate language must be painstakingly and laboriously acquired.

To those of us, on the other hand, who encounter the law as litigants or defendants, law presents itself as a closed system that needs to be interpreted for us and to us. In a real and even unremarkable sense, the language of the law is not our language.

So here is another plane of rupture: in the first place, the '*langue*' of law is in retreat from the normal flux of being and becoming in the social domain. Now, and still in the social domain, we find a priestly caste who, interpreting the law to us, are also by virtue of the same process possessors of the special domain of the law, a reserved mystery from which, *sans* interpreters, we are necessarily excluded.

Now the purpose of law is, of course, the ordering and regulation of society. You might say law is the means by which social relations enter into the domain of form, and the opposite of form is chaos. Any one individual might, from time to time, be able to live with a certain amount of chaos in the day to day; we have long since learned that society without laws will rapidly descend into, as Hobbes puts it, 'a ceaseless war of all against all'. This does not mean, however, that the boundary can ever be fixed or definite; we should think of it as a tide line, perhaps, a definite frontier whose line is always, to a certain small degree, in doubt.

It happens that social order in a normal social democracy is founded in law, and law is founded in, has its being in, language. The particular forms in language we use to contain the vital energies of lawgiving are few, and aspire to the immutable. Rhetorically, they tend to the declarative and, inside those parameters, towards the twin dynamics of permitting and forbidding. In this particular sense, the language of law is a kind of written and spoken organised withdrawal from history – in the sense that history as we live it consists of the unregulated and protean arrival of new facts from the future, and law is a permanent attempt to govern the present from the safety of the past.

You may well sense by now the uneasy ghost of Plato hovering offstage, rehearsing his lines in a worried murmur. Plato considered that reality, though he would not have used the term, is vertically structured, with the ideal forms at the top of the pyramid, the reality quotient of phenomena becoming thinner and more diluted as we descend all the way down to the muddled level of the everyday. In Plato's world view our task as humans desirous of becoming enlightened is to work our way by reason and clarity of thought upwards out of the fog into the rarefied empyrean, the high clear air of the ideal forms.

The higher we get, of course, the closer we approach to the Ideal Forms, the more measured our thoughts and our language become. We seek, then, the absolute, the frozen, the fixed and definite, that which is out of time – and to the extent that humans are capable of participating in this sacred order, it must be by virtue of language that itself remains unchanging. You might say, in Plato's world it is indeed possible, at least thinkable, to have the final word.

This divine achievement is, of course, reserved in our fallen world for the most exalted judges alone – but then as so many of their lordships will tell you, like the Gods of Olympus, their lordships, axiomatically, are never wrong.

If it were merely the case that the language of law and the language of society are at all times in a state of tension, that would not be so bad, provided of course that this tension could be constituted as a living dialectic. This, unfortunately, is far from the case. The process is, in fact, asymmetric: laws accumulate, and as they accumulate, so the power of the state accumulates. As the power of the state accumulates, the social space for unencumbered action necessarily contracts. As the space for free action contracts, so *parole* turns mutinous, retreats from the sphere of the state, grows and mutates under pressure from the constantly arriving future. Eventually, a schism is created between the state and its language, on the one hand, and the people with its multiplicity of *paroles* on the other. Just as asymmetry in wealth and power generates a social chasm, so, too, this social chasm is reflected in the gap between *langue* and *parole*, or, as it then becomes, the gap between the language of the state and the languages of the people.

I do not mean here that the language of the state is a professional dialect, of the kind that tends naturally to grow in any defined profession. The medical profession has its dialect, its shorthand; so, too, does engineering, shipping, policing, factory work, teaching and so on. It's an inherent tendency in language to exfoliate in specialist vocabularies and patterns, habits, of usage. But such occupational dialects are no more than *paroles* of kinship, subsets of the wider shared *parole* of a given society at a given time.

That there is a dialect peculiar to all who work in the law, many of us have observed; and in so far as this is a normal, a conventional thing, it is a harmless phenomenon.

The problem arises when this specialist dialect forms a particular relationship to the language of law as deployed by the state. In effect, it leads to the emergence or creation of a caste whose private domain is the law – in brute terms, to a common interest between lawgivers and interpreters of the law, which acts, over time, to increase the alienation of the citizen from the law, and hence from the state.

It comes to the point where a small but powerful consortium of interests comes to identify itself with the language of law, and hence to identify the law with itself. This caste, I should say, is not confined to the lawyers, judges and lawmakers; as the state class grows, its language begins to metamorphose into the language of politics, more precisely the language of governance. Not the laws themselves, to be sure, but those particular and specific habits of language – with this profound difference: where the language of law attempts to enshrine concrete concepts, definable precepts and principles, the language of the state tends towards emptiness, towards an illusory ideal of the state as instrument and embodiment of achievable total control.

This growth outward from law continues and makes terrible the already evacuated relationship between personhood and the language of law; just as the actual citizen, the individual whose consent is notionally necessary for governance to have authority, is nowhere present as himself or herself in the codex of laws, so also that individual ceases to be real in the edicts of governance. Thus a citizen patient in a hospital becomes a customer of the health service, and the civil servant, employed by us acting in common in order to serve us as citizens, discovers that in fact she serves the state, and that the citizen standing before her is no longer a citizen person but a customer, a client, a cipher in the calculus of state management.

What begins as a notion of necessary austerity in language develops a dark twin, a merciless and instrumental language of governance. This process, of course, is not confined to the upper echelons of the state, to the lawmakers and lawgivers: it attracts its adherents and cheerleaders – some of them, the Gardaí, say, the upper echelons of the defence forces and the upper reaches of the civil service, by reason of professional contiguity, but others, too, by reason of appetite or affinity, including political journalists and commentators, academics, and – not least of these parasites on power – persons of wealth and standing having a vested interest in closeness to the state.

I began by saying that law is a directive arising from desire, embodied in language. In our system, the desire may crystallise in one of three places: the courts might decide that an existing law is inadequate in its relation to a particular circumstance, and require of the Oireachtas that it remedy a deficiency by amendment, or that it cause a new law to be written to meet the circumstance; the Oireachtas, more practically the cabinet, might cause a law to be written for a specific purpose in order that it be passed by the Oireachtas; or, in obedience to an obligation arising from EU member-ship or other international affiliation, the Oireachtas might cause a law to be written, and subsequently enacted, in accordance with or in fulfilment of that obligation.

The actual writing of the law, the embodiment of desire as a directive in language, is the task of the parliamentary drafts-men and women.

These men and women are heavily constrained by prece-dent, in other words by custom and tradition. They will, in-evitably, turn inward to the language of existing law for their vocabulary, syntax and grammar. They will strive for a cold lucidity; they will strive to eliminate any and all possible ambiguities of meaning; they will reach for a language that has no home in our hearts or in our daily speech, a language whose permanent tropism is towards the imagined cold per-fection of the idealised unchanging state.

This process takes place within the civil service, notionally a body of men and women employed, as the name implies, to serve the *civis*, that is, to serve the people. The more proper name, at this point in our evolution as a republic, would be the state service. In the *Irish Times* on 22 April 2011, Eddie Molloy contributed a fascinating article, the core argument of which was that 'The country desperately needs a techni-cally qualified, ethical, accountable public service, one that will place the public good ahead of the preferences of the incumbent government whenever officials are faced with hard choices between the two.' Mr Molloy, as he plainly states, does not believe that we have such a service at present.

I agree with him, of course, as any sane person would, but I do not underestimate the difficulties that root-and-branch reform will encounter should we ever embark on that course, not least the difficulty of transforming the habits of speech and writing, by which I mean the habits of thought, that permeate the state service.

And these habits, this habitual stance in language, are deep-rooted. In 1975, the poet Michael Hartnett, in Section 4 of 'A Farewell to English' wrote:

> So we queued up at the Castle
> in nineteen-twenty-two
> to make our Gaelic
> or our Irish dream come true.
> We could have from that start
> made certain of our fate
> but we chose to learn the noble art
> of writing forms in triplicate.
> With big wide eyes
> and childish smiles
> quivering on our lips
> we entered the Irish paradise
> of files and paper-clips.

Such is the flexibility, the multivalence of language in the service of poetry that no reader will take this as a literal description, but few will fail to recognise what Hartnett describes and most of us will understand very well what he means. The 'Irish paradise of files and paper-clips' is the Four Courts as much as it is the Department of Finance; it is in any case a vivid invoking of the state as we the citizens encounter it.

Hartnett's poem is, of course, cast in a very different register of language, a register in which allusion, affective use of words, colour and tone are deployed to evocative effect as spurs to the imagination. His language is, in a word, passionate.

Aristotle tells us that 'the law is reason free from passion', and just as we wish our laws to be reasonable, so also we would wish them uninflected by some transitory passion. Our laws, almost all of them, are at the very least reasonable – and therein lies a considerable difficulty, for, as Aristotle also reminds us, 'Whereas the law is passionless, passion must ever sway the heart of man.'

Some passions are of the moment, and often it is a good thing that we do not take steps to act on those passions in the civic arena. But there is such a thing as shaped and controlled passion; there are passions that need to be actively encouraged, and constantly renewed – the passion for justice, for instance, for equity, for liberty.

Our problem is this: how do we frame our laws and governance so that the dry bones of the law and the day-to-day tedium of the state's ordinary business are constantly animated by these and other desirable civic passions?

In a settled society, provided the laws are reasonable and provided the state acts always within the law, momentary random dissatisfactions can be subsumed into the overall sway of things.

But, as we build up the corpus of law and the habitual behaviour of the state on the one hand, dissatisfactions begin to accumulate on the other side of the scales in equal measure, so that the state tends inevitably to withdraw farther and farther into its citadel of language, into a condition of mind engendered by the increasing remoteness of its perfected language – and the farther the state withdraws, the more we begin to distrust it.

In confronting the state through its laws and in that denatured language of governance which derives from the desiccated language of the laws, the citizen is denied not only his naive belief that law, and hence the state, is concerned with justice; he is denied, perhaps more fundamentally, a relationship with the state in which passion can find expression in dialogue. He or she finds that there is no pulse at the heart of the state, no governing passion restrained by moderation in language. Where there was once the fiery and passionate dream and promise of a republic, now there is only an arid landscape, picked over by weary souls who, perhaps unknowingly, are constantly tempted genuinely to despise us for our native dreams – above all, for our naive belief that the state exists for the promotion of the common good.

When Hartnett says, 'We could have from that start/made certain of our fate', he is saying a great deal. Among other things he is reminding us that our infant republic, at the handing over of power, could have chosen differently, could have looked beyond the inherited practice of civil administration, the inherited apparatus of law and its customs of governance; but of course we did no such thing. We took on, unquestioned, the burden of the common law as it had evolved in Britain, with all its precedents and preconceptions, never once asking if this was an appropriate tradition for our people, in our time. Never once asking if this was the proper frame for our future. We took on the British civil service tradition, not just in its forms of management and administration but in its entire suffocating weight of custom and practice. The beggars, to invoke Yeats, changed places indeed, but for the majority of the population the lash went on. Now there might well have been sound pragmatic reasons for doing this as a temporary measure, if only to buttress a fragile new Free State by providing it with an administrative apparatus in a time of transition, in a time of war. But of course this isn't what happened. We embraced the Irish paradise, its files, paper-clips and language, with relish. And stopped there.

For the vast majority of people, the harp replaced the crown on police stations and on the letterheads of the state – and that was all. There was no pretence that the state would be founded on consultation with the people, no attempt to conduct and direct a broad-ranging first-principles public debate on what form the state should take, what values its laws and its legislature should embody and profess. The passion of revolution, such as it was, found itself quietly extinguished in a decisive manoeuvre by a managerial class many of whom were already waiting and poised in the wings.

When I say with Hartnett that 'we embraced the Irish paradise', I should perhaps qualify that 'we'; the truth is, of course, that with residual exceptions, the architects of our new state were in the main second-generation revolutionaries and enduring functionaries of the previous administration. We forget or elide a simple but profound truth: the War of Independence was conducted largely by the urban and rural poor, officered and led in the main by the lower middle class. The lawgivers and managers of the new Free State were cut from a different cloth; they edged out the rough men with a practised ease, as is always the case. First come the dreamers and poets, and the poor who do the fighting and dying; then come the smooth men, the silky judges and lawyers and administrators. And, of course, behind these respectable men, the hard-eyed executioners when they are needed.

In time, those of the revolutionary generation who survived into politics had the hard edges sanded off them by the ceaseless murmuring abrasions of what was in essence an unaltered and seemingly insurmountable process of governance. As the Normans became *Hiberniores Hibernii*, so too the men and women who had overthrown imperial rule made themselves comfortable in the corridors and in the assured language of enduring functional power. Prisoners of the unaltered and unaltering state.

There was, there remains to this day, a sense of helplessness at the heart of government. As if stasis were fore-ordained and inescapable.

In his magnificent book-length poem *The Rough Field*, published in 1972, John Montague sets up a kind of counterpoint to his own words, a recurring series of quotations that question and inflect his own imaginings.

Two of these are set one above the other, by way of introducing the section entitled 'Patriotic Suite', first published by the Dolmen Press as a pamphlet in 1966. The first is from poet and ethnic-cleanser Edmund Spenser, speaking of Ireland: 'They say it is the Fatal Destiny of that land, that no purposes whatsoever which are meant for her good will prosper.' It is a perception to chill the blood, inasmuch as its prophetic power, whatever its provenance, rings as true today as it did during the barbarous Elizabethan conquest.

Spenser, who gives no authority for this fatalistic observation, was of course sent to rule over a sizeable portion of the province of Munster, and did a pretty good job of ensuring that neither the good nor the people prospered under his steely eye.

The second quotation is from Friedrich Engels: 'The real aims of a revolution, those which are not illusions, are always

to be realised after that revolution.' If there were revolutionary aspirations in the Rising and in the War of Independence,
I would argue that they were quickly suffocated in the lore,
language and precedents of that *mentalité* of governance we
so easily and unquestioningly took on ourselves.

It is a truism, and often by recent commentators held
against them, that the revolutionaries of our proto-republic
were visionaries and romantics – as if this were self-evidently
a bad thing. In so far as visionaries and romantics embarked
on revolution are more likely to be driven by song, story and
poem than by political analysis, there is a certain sting in the
charge. But without Davis and Ferguson, and behind them Ó
Rathaille, Ó Súilleabháin, Ó Bruadair and the anonymous
makers of the song tradition, how should we have risen, how
should we have struck, as we did, for liberty? Where, in a
phrase, should we have found that passion of the heart? The
great singer Frank Harte once observed that the winners write
the histories and the losers make the songs – without those
songs, poems and stories, how should we have remembered
ourselves, how should we have formulated a better dream of
who we yet might be?

It is a pity that Pearse, McDonagh, Collins, de Valera and
Markievicz were not well versed in the theoretical projection
of the post-revolutionary future; it is a tragedy that the only
revolutionary theorist among those freedom fighters came to
his end prematurely, strapped to a chair in the execution yard
of Kilmainham Gaol.

Well, our republic was not arrived at by a process of cold
reasoning. Yeats might well have nurtured, for a brief while,
the hope that England would keep faith, and we have many
among us who persist in that fond delusion still, but the
Rising happened, the War of Independence happened, and we

are the direct inheritors of those irrevocable, inescapable passionate gestures.

Julius Caesar had sage advice for revolutionaries: 'If you must break the law, do it to seize power: in all other cases observe it.' Ireland's tragedy is that, having broken the law to seize power, we immediately reinstated that very law we had overthrown. There is no more poignant symbol of this self-defeating revolution than Collins commanding those borrowed batteries that shelled the Four Courts. We live with that legacy still, and whether or not we aim to reform or refound our republic, we would do well to square up to this monumental fact.

In Section 4 of 'a Patriotic Suite' Montague celebrates the nobility of the founding dream:

Symbolic depth charge of music
Releases a national dream;
From clerk to paladin
In a single violent day.
Files of men from shattered buildings
(Slouch hat, blunt mauser gun)
Frame the freedom that they won.

The bread queue, the messianic
Agitator of legend
Arriving on the train –
Christ and socialism –
Wheatfield and factory
Vivid in the sun;
Connolly's dream, if any one.

But Montague is too good, too true a poet, to leave it at that. He goes on in the third and final stanza to say this:

All revolutions are interior
The displacement of spirit
By the arrival of fact,
Ceaseless as cloud across sky,
Sudden as sun.
Movement of a butterfly
Modifies everything.

The revolution that we never had is that interior revolution. Because we did not change in our spirits, nothing of any substance was ever displaced by the arrival of a new set of facts. We failed, if I might put it very simply indeed, to change our minds.

We failed to change our language.

In the poems and the songs and stories there are more durable maps of memory than in all the edicts of the state. Perhaps we need to find new ways to re-insert these memories in our narrative of who we most deeply and truly are?

I would not underestimate the difficulty. In her poem 'A Child's Map of Dublin' (1991), Paula Meehan's opening stanza charts an exclusion process that has only accelerated since Montague wrote 'Patriotic Suite':

I wanted to find you Connolly's Starry Plough,
the flag I have lived under since birth or since
I first scanned nightskies and learned the nature of work.
'That hasn't been on show in years,' the porter told us.
They're revising at the National Museum,

all hammers and drills and dust, conversion to
an interpretive centre in the usual contemporary style.

I believe that our present crisis stems from a double failure:
the failure of the revolutionary generation to establish a true
republic, and our inevitable consequent ongoing failure to
imagine a new state from inside the facts and the language of
the present state.

Hannah Arendt says:

Predictions of the future are never anything but projec-
tions of present automatic processes and procedures, that
is, of occurrences that are likely to come to pass if men do
not act and if nothing unexpected happens; every action,
for better or worse, and every accident necessarily
destroys the whole pattern in whose frame the prediction
moves and where it finds its evidence.

Change, in other words, meaningful change, will require some
considerable accident or some profound, history-breaking
action.

As with predictions, so with proposals: projected solutions
couched in the present language of politics can at best offer a
kind of battlefield triage to keep the patient alive for the
moment. The real problem is to find a mould-breaking
gesture, a departure into some new language, which offers a
whole new life, perhaps a whole new kind of life, for the
patient.

If we are to imagine a new republic, we are constrained to
do so from outside the walls of the state – and we would do
well to remind ourselves of Bob Dylan's useful phrase: 'To live
outside the law you must be honest.'

The language of public life in Ireland today is a language of subservience to authority when it is not a bullying on the part of the state. Cringing before the displeasure of our new colonial masters, our governments have inflicted on us suffering and sacrifice into the fourth or fifth generation so that a political and banking system brutally indifferent to our needs and desires may be saved from its own excesses.

Dress it how you like, neither the last nor the present government can credibly claim that its first, governing loyalty is to the people of Ireland.

I think again of Michael Hartnett, and his excoriating, prophetic vision:

I saw our governments the other night –
I think the scene was Leopardstown –
horribly deformed dwarfs rode the racetrack
each mounted on a horribly deformed dwarf;
greenfaced, screaming, yellow-toothed, prodding
each other with electric prods, thrashing
each other's skinny arses, dribbling snot
and smeared with their own dung, they galloped
towards the prize, a glass and concrete anus.

I think the result was a dead heat.

Not, I agree, the language of statecraft or diplomacy – but a living language, a language capable of telling and carrying truths. A language far closer to the truth of what is than any number of government press releases, or post-ministerial *mea culpa*s.

I doubt that I need to, but perhaps I had better make it explicit that I am not suggesting for a moment that the language of law can ever be spoken or written as poetry is spoken and written. I do want to say, forcibly, that unless the language of governance breaks with the dead weight of the language of law and moves decisively closer to the fully inclusive *paroles* of song, poem and story, then the gap between governor and governed can only, and surely must, become that deep chasm out of which chaos will come swaggering one dark night.

Poetry is, among other things, passion embodied in living language; there is room for reason, and for unreason, too, but above all else poetry is disciplined language in the register of human passions. Poetry is the living language raised to the power of imagination.

Is it beyond us to found a dialogue between state and people in a living language?

The poet's business is with the dignity of the human soul in language, and whether it be the hard tyranny of persecution or the soft, insidious tyranny of willed indifference, the one thing government from above will not abide is language that insists on the irreducible human dignity of the citizen.

If the language of governance, and hence the practice and obligations of government, derive from the inherited corpus of law, and if the language of law derives from and gains its authority from the language of the constitution, and if you grant me that piecemeal reform is little more than a holding action in the face of looming chaos, then our task is a very simple one: we must rewrite the constitution.

We must change our language.

It has been done before, in a post-colonial state; it has been done, it is being done, in our time.

In post-apartheid South Africa, they faced up to the challenge of a new jurisprudence as a concomitant of facing up to imagining a new politics.

In a landmark case concerning the issue of whether or not certain benefits should be extended to Mozambican refugees, Justice Yvonne Mokgoro introduced, in parallel with the Kantian ideal of 'the Kingdom of Ends', the concept of *ubuntu*. The word translates, more or less, as 'humaneness', according to the scholar Drucilla Cornell, on whose description of that landmark judgment I am drawing here. Cornell tells us that Mokgoro stated the following:

> Generally, *ubuntu* translates as *humaneness*. In its most fundamental sense, it translates as personhood and morality. Metaphorically, it expresses itself in *umuntu ngumuntu ngabantu*, describing the significance of group solidarity on survival issues so central to the survival of communities. While it envelops the key values of group solidarity, compassion, respect, human dignity, conformity to basic norms and collective unity, in its fundamental sense it denoted humanity and morality. Its spirit emphasises respect for human dignity, marking a shift from confrontation to conciliation.

In a later part of the judgment, Justice Mokgoro goes on to say: 'In the Western cultural heritage, respect and the value for life, manifested in the all-embracing concepts of *humanity* and *menswaardigheit* are also highly priced.'

Cornell brings two towering figures to our attention, Justice Mokgoro and the former Constitutional Court Judge, Justice Laurie Ackermann, champion of the proposal that human rights are grounded in the moral idea of dignity, itself an idea he derives from German idealism. Between them, if I understand Cornell here, they can be said to propose a synthesis, a co-existence, between the rights of the individual and the rights of community; both ideas, says Cornell, 'appeal to the principle of humanity as the basis of legality'.

It is not without significance, I think, that this new jurisprudence feels free to draw on the plurality of languages available to the new state. It is not without significance that the new South Africa is respectful in its postures towards both the old and the new, towards high culture, including elements of the inherited legal culture of the former state, and towards the demotic cultures of the powerless.

The choice, as these learned judges recognise, is to make it new or to fall back into the disempowering language of the former regime.

To step outside your language is to step into a particular liberty; it is also to experience that vertigo, familiar to the poet, that Michael Hartnett expressed when he wrote: 'I have poems to hand, it's words I cannot find.' I would not deny the difficulty of what I am proposing. The language we employ in all its registers is overwhelmingly an inherited language, and the very fact that the language of law endures as it does suggests that to some extent at least it possesses an adequacy, an aptness for its purpose, that we should take very seriously into consideration. It is not as if, by will and *fiat*, we can imagine a wholly new language into existence – but that is by no means what I am suggesting. The task is to find and imagine a register in language that steps between liberty and vertigo, that conserves what serves and provides, it may be, for states of mind and being that we are only beginning to imagine. Above all else, perhaps, a register of language that embodies and renders active a reconciliation between passion and reason.

So, very simply, we must find the words. The old words will not do. The old language must be mined and sifted for what is good in it, and there will be a great deal, I am sure. But, only so much of what has brought us here will serve.

Lawyer and politician, poet and citizen, we face a common task. To build a right republic we must find the right words.

References

'DO YOU KNOW WHAT A REPUBLIC IS?': THE ADVENTURE AND
MISADVENTURES OF AN IDEA
Fintan O'Toole

1 *Irish Times*, 19 November 2011.
2 *Irish Times*, 2 March 2012.
3 *Irish Review* (Dublin), vol. 3, no. 29 (July 1913), pp. 217–27.
4 *Irish Worker*, 22 August 1914; *Workers' Republic*, 18 March 1916.
5 Brian Cowen, speech at Georgetown University, Washington DC, 21 March 2012.
6 Ernest Renan, *The Poetry of the Celtic Races and Other Studies*, translated by William G. Hutchison [1896], Kennikat Press, Port Washington, New York, 1970, pp. 66–75.
7 Dáil Éireann debates, vol. 1, 21 January 1919.
8 *Irish Times*, 5 June 1935.
9 *New York Times*, 31 October 1937.
10 James Loughlin, *The British Monarchy and Ireland*, Cambridge University Press, 2007, p. 345.
11 Elizabeth Keane, *An Irish Statesman and Revolutionary*, I.B. Tauris, London, 2006, p. 52.
12 'An Irishman's Diary', *Irish Times*, 19 April 1949.
13 Thomas Paine, *The Works of Thomas Paine, Esq.*, London, 1792, p. 105.
14 Maurizio Viroli, *Republicanism*, Hill & Wang, New York, 2002.
15 Edward Stillingfleet Cayley, *The European Revolutions of 1848*, Smith, Elder & Co., London, 1856.
16 Quoted in Viroli, *Republicanism*, p. 89.

17 Viroli, *Republicanism*, p. 12–13.
18 Joe Lee, *Ireland 1912–1985: Politics and Society*, Cambridge University Press, 1989, p. 646.
19 Heinrich Böll, *Irish Journal*, Northwestern University Press, Evanston, IL, 1994, pp. 109–10.
20 John Cooney, *John Charles McQuaid: Ruler of Catholic Ireland*, O'Brien Press, Dublin, 1999, p. 97.
21 I make these arguments myself in *Ship of Fools*, Faber and Faber, London, 2009.
22 P. W. Joyce, *English As We Speak It in Ireland*, M. H. Gill & Son, Dublin, 1910, p. 312.

THE REPUBLIC AS A TRADITION AND AN IDEAL IN IRELAND TODAY
Iseult Honohan

1 James Harrington, *The Commonwealth of Oceana and A System of Politics* [1656], Cambridge University Press, 1992, p. 8.
2 Philip Pettit, *Republicanism* [1997], Oxford University Press, 1999, p. 71.
3 Hannah Arendt, *The Human Condition*, Anchor Books, New York, 1958, p. 210.
4 Niccolò Machiavelli, *The Discourses* [1531], edited by Bernard Crick, Penguin, Harmondsworth, 1983, p. 253.
5 For example, Tom Garvin, 'An Irish republican tradition?' in Iseult Honohan (ed.), *Republicanism in Ireland: Confronting Theories and Traditions*, Manchester University Press, 2008.
6 Margaret O'Callaghan, 'Reconsidering the republican tradition in nineteenth-century Ireland', in Honohan (ed.), *Republicanism in Ireland*.
7 Cécile Laborde, *Critical Republicanism, The Hijab Controversy and Political Philosophy*, Oxford University Press, 2008; Iseult Honohan, 'Tolerance and non-domination' in Jan Dobbernack and Tariq Modood (eds.), *Hard to Accept: New Perspectives on Tolerance, Intolerance and Respect*, forthcoming.
8 James Bohman, *Democracy Across Borders: From Demos to Demoi*, MIT Press, Boston, MA, 2007; Máire Brophy, *Intervention and Sovereignty: A Republican Approach*, unpublished Ph.D. thesis, University College Dublin.

9 Margaret Canovan, 'Trust the people! Populism and the two faces of democracy', *Political Studies*, no. 47 (March 1999), pp. 2–16.

10 Cécile Laborde, 'The Culture(s) of the Republic. Nationalism and multiculturalism in French Republican Thought', *Political Theory*, no. 29 (October 2001), pp. 716–35; Laborde, *Critical Republicanism*.

CIVIC VIRTUE, AUTONOMY AND RELIGIOUS SCHOOLS: WHAT WOULD MACHIAVELLI DO?
Tom Hickey

1 For a more complete account of liberty as non-domination, see Iseult Honohan's contribution to this volume.

2 The scholarship associated with Quentin Skinner, Philip Pettit and others is often referred to as neo-republicanism. See for instance, Philip Pettit, *Republicanism: A Theory of Freedom and Government*, Oxford University Press, 1997; Quentin Skinner, *Liberty before Liberalism*, Cambridge University Press, 1998.

3 Machiavelli suggested that 'just as good morals, if they are to be maintained, have need of the laws, so the laws, if they are to be observed, have need of good morals'. See Niccolò Machiavelli, *The Complete Works and Others*, ed. and trans. Allan Gilbert, Duke University Press, Durham, NC, 1965, p. 493.

4 Will Kymlicka is one who objects to civic republicanism on this basis. He insists that 'civic republicanism refers to the view that the best life – the most truly human life – is one which privileges political participation over other spheres of human endeavour . . . [I]t is inconsistent with liberalism's commitment to pluralism, and in any event is implausible as a general account of the good life for all persons.' Will Kymlicka, *Politics in the Vernacular: Nationalism, Multiculturalism, and Citizenship*, Oxford University Press, 2001, p. 297 n. 6.

5 See John Rawls, *Political Liberalism*, Columbia University Press, New York, 1996.

6 For an interesting overview from a republican perspective, see Cécile Laborde, *Critical Republicanism: The Hijab Controversy and Political Philosophy*, Oxford University Press, 2008.

7 These were the words of Bernard Stasi, President of the Commission, as quoted by Laborde. Ibid., n. 133.

8 The dissident republican intellectual Séan O'Faoláin decried this
   approach in the literary periodical *The Bell* in the 1940s. See Séan
   O'Faoláin, 'To What Possible Future', *The Bell*, April 1942,
   pp. 1–9, as quoted in Mark McNally, 'Séan O'Faoláin's Discourse
   of "The Betrayal of the Republic" in Mid-Twentieth Century
   Ireland', in Jeremy Jennings and Iseult Honohan (eds.), *Republicanism in Theory and Practice*, Routledge, London, 2005,
   pp. 79–94.

9 This view is associated in particular with Aristotle. John Rawls
   draws a distinction between the civic republicanism of Machiavelli and de Tocqueville on the one hand and Aristotelian 'civic
   humanism' on the other. He claims the former to be compatible
   with his political liberalism (i.e. 'neutral' between conceptions of
   the good life) while the latter understands 'man as a social, even
   political, animal whose essential nature is most fully realised in a
   democratic society' and accordingly takes political participation
   to be 'the privileged locus of the good life'. See Rawls, *Political
   Liberalism*, p. 206.

10 Neo-republican scholars such as Pettit and Skinner would distance
   themselves from this Aristotelianism, and draw a distinction
   between so-called neo-Roman and neo-Athenian republicanism.

11 See Iseult Honohan, 'Educating Citizens: Nation-Building and its
   Republican Limits', in Jennings and Honohan (eds.), *Republicanism in Theory and Practice*, pp. 199–207, which has influenced
   my ideas in this area. Honohan develops these themes in her
   contribution to this volume.

12 Honohan further argues in this vein that virtuous republican citizens must expand their perceptions to become aware of 'multiply
   reiterated interdependencies'. This requires citizens to understand
   the broader social and political arrangements within which they
   live their lives and enjoy their liberty. This involves 'countering
   assumptions of individual self-sufficiency and misconceptions
   about the impact of government and the effects of non-participa-
   tion'. See Honohan, 'Educating Citizens', p. 205.

13 Machiavelli believed that the different factions that gained power
   'never organised [Florence] for the common benefit, but always
   for the advantage of their own party' which led to an absence
   of shared political trust, and ultimately, domination. See
   Machiavelli, *The Complete Works*, p. 296.

14 Sara Shumer, 'Republican Politics and its Corruption', *Political Theory*, vol. 7 no. 1 (February 1979), pp. 15–16.

15 On the idea of public reason, see John Rawls, *The Law of Peoples: with 'The Idea of Public Reason Revisited'*, Harvard University Press, Cambridge, MA, 2001, pp. 131–80.

16 Rawls explains the idea with the simple illustration of Servetus, who 'could understand why Calvin wanted to burn him at the stake'. Similarly it is understandable why some or many individuals might want to coerce other individuals on the basis of their own innermost beliefs, but it is a different matter for those other individuals to reasonably accept those reasons as legitimate.

17 *Mozert v. Hawkins County Board of Education*, 827 F.2d 1058 (6th Cir.1987).

18 For analysis of the case in light of civic education in the liberal state see, Stephen Macedo, *Diversity and Distrust: Civic Education in a Multicultural Democracy*, Harvard University Press, Cambridge, MA, 2000, pp. 157–65.

19 *Mozert*, p. 1062.

20 Rawls, *Political Liberalism*, p. 200.

21 This distinction, which is so fundamental to the argument made by neo-republicans, is discussed widely in the literature. For a comprehensive analysis, See Philip Pettit, 'Law and Liberty', in Samantha Besson and Jose Marti (eds.), *Legal Republicanism: National and International Perspectives*, Oxford University Press, 2009, pp. 39–59.

22 Eamonn Callan, *Creating Citizens: Political Education and Liberal Democracy*, Oxford University Press, 1997, pp. 152–61.

23 Ibid., p. 153.

24 Ibid.

25 Ibid., pp. 153–4.

26 Steven Macedo makes this argument, but from the standpoint of political liberalism rather than republicanism. See Stephen Macedo, 'Liberal Civic Education and Religious Fundamentalism: The Case of God v. John Rawls?', *Ethics*, vol. 105 no. 3 (April 1995), pp. 468–96.

27 Its report, published in May 2012, is to inform the reforms that are to take place in school patronage in the coming years. For a brief critique, see Tom Hickey, 'A Thought Experiment for Ruari Quinn' at www.humanrights.ie (accessed August 2012).

28 See *Information on Areas for Possible Divesting of Patronage of Primary Schools*, Department of Education and Skills, Dublin, 2010.

29 On this argument, see chapters 4 and 5 of Eoin Daly, *Religion, Law and the Irish State*, Clarus, Dublin, 2012. See also Eoin Daly and Tom Hickey, 'Religious freedom and the "right to discriminate" in the school admissions context: a neo-republican critique', *Legal Studies*, vol. 31 no. 4 (December 2011), pp. 615–43.

30 Aristotle, *Nicomachean Ethics*, trans. Terence Irwin, Hackett, Indianapolis, IN, 1985, p. 35.

31 The most recent figures suggest that 87 per cent of those living in Ireland describe themselves as Catholic. See Central Statistics Office, *Census Reports: Population classified by religion for relevant censuses from 1881–2006*, Central Statistics Office, Dublin, 2006.

32 I am guided on these arguments by the work of Ian MacMullen. See Ian MacMullen, *Faith in Schools? Autonomy, Citizenship and Religious Education in the Liberal State*, Princeton University Press, NJ, 2007, pp. 169–75.

33 On this issue, see Tom Hickey, 'Domination and the Hijab in Irish Schools', *Dublin University Law Journal*, vol. 31 (2009), pp. 127–53.

34 This point is made by Ian MacMullen.

CITIZENS OR SUBJECTS? CIVIL SOCIETY AND THE REPUBLIC
Fred Powell

1 Charles Baxter, 'Behind Murakami's Mirror', in *New York Review of Books*, 6 December 2011, pp. 23–5.

2 John Ehrenberg, *Civil Society*, New York University Press, NY, 1999, p. 91.

3 Jonathan I. Israel, *Radical Enlightenment*, Oxford University Press, 2001, p. 259.

4 Russ Leo, 'Caute: Jonathan Israel's Secular Modernity', *Journal for Cultural and Religious Theory*, vol. 9 no. 2 (summer 2008), p. 76.

5 Ibid., p. 77.

6 Israel, *Radical Enlightenment*, p. 285.

7 Ibid., pp. 295–327.

8   Jonathan I. Israel, *The Revolutionary Mind*, University of Princeton Press, NJ, 2010, pp. 180–85.

9   Nicholas Phillipson, *Adam Smith: An Enlightened Life*, Allen Lane, London, 2010, p. 157.

10   Ehrenberg, *Civil Society*, p. 96.

11   Fred Powell, 'Civil Society Theory: Paine', in Helmut K. Anheier, Stefan Toepler and Regina List (eds.), *International Encyclopaedia of Civil Society*, vol. 1, Springer, New York, 2010, pp. 438–42.

12   David Dwan, *The Great Community*, Field Day, Dublin, 2008, p. 14.

13   John Keane, *Tom Paine: A Political Life*, Bloomsbury, London, 1995, p. 324.

14   Alexis de Tocqueville, *Democracy in America*, ed. Richard D. Heftner, Mentor, New York, 1956, p. 202.

15   Howard Zinn, *A People's History of the United States*, HarperCollins, New York, 1999, p. 218.

16   Dwan, *The Great Community*, pp. 63–5.

17   Cited in Chris Hann and Elizabeth Dunn (eds.), *Civil Society: Challenging Western Models*, Routledge, London, 1996, p. 4.

18   Antonio Gramsci, *Selections from Prison Notebooks*, ed. Quintin Hoare and Geoffrey Nowell-Smith, Lawrence and Wishart, London, 1971, p. 12.

19   Hann and Dunn, *Civil Society*, p. 5.

20   Ibid., p. 8.

21   David G. Anderson, 'Bringing Civil Society to an Uncivilised Place: Citizenship Regimes in Russia's Arctic Frontier', in Hann and Dunn (eds.), *Civil Society*, p. 99.

22   Ibid., p. 100.

23   Fred Powell, *The Politics of Civil Society: Neoliberalism or Social Left?*, Policy, Bristol, 2007, p. 206.

24   Jean L. Cohen and Andrew Arato, *Civil Society and Political Theory*, MIT Press, Cambridge, MA, 1992.

25   Ibid., p. 9.

26   Harold Pinter, *Art, Truth, Politics*, Nobel Lecture, 2005.

27   *Guardian*, 8 December 2005.

28   John Keane, *The Life and Death of Democracy*, Simon and Schuster, London, 2009.

29   Benjamin Barber, *Strong Democracy: Participatory Politics for*

a New Age, University of California Press, Berkeley, CA, 1984, p. xvii.

30 Ibid., p. 20.

31 Thomas Prugh, Robert Constanza and Herman Daly, *The Local Politics of Global Sustainability*, Island Press, Washington, DC, 2000, p. 10.

32 Ibid. p. 220.

33 Iris Marion Young, *Inclusion and Democracy*, Oxford University Press, 2000, pp. 9–10.

34 Ibid., p. 54.

35 Ibid., p. 55.

36 Bill Cooke and Uma Kothari (eds.), *Participation: The New Tyranny*, Zed Books, London, 2001.

37 J. P. O'Carroll, 'Cultural Lag and Democratic Deficit in Ireland', *Community Development Journal* 37 (1) (January 2002), pp. 10–19.

38 Clifford Geertz, *The Interpretation of Culture*, Huntington, London, 1975.

39 Ferdinand Tonnies, *Community and Association*, Routledge and Kegan Paul, London, 1955.

40 Terence Brown, *Ireland a Social and Cultural History*, Fontana, London, 1981, p. 41.

41 Patrick Macklem, 'Militant Democracy, Legal Pluralism, and the Paradox of Self-determination', *International Journal of Constitutional Law*, vol. 4 no. 3 (July 2006), p. 488.

42 Fred Powell, *The Politics of Irish Social Policy 1600–1999*, Edwin Mellen Press, New York, 1992.

43 Fred Powell and Martin Geoghegan, *The Politics of Community Development*, A. & A. Farmar, Dublin, 2004, p. 17.

44 Gerald Delanty, 'Modernity and Postmodernity', in Austin Harrington (ed.), *Modern Social Theory*, Oxford University Press, 2005, p. 276.

45 Cited in Samuel Huntington, *The Clash of Civilizations*, Simon and Schuster, London, 2002, p. 306.

46 Tariq Ali, *The Clash of Fundamentalisms*, Verso, London, 2002, pp. 3–4.

47 Michael D. Higgins, *Renewing the Republic*, Liberties Press, Dublin, 2011, p. 21.

48 Ibid., p. 22.

49 Ibid., p. 62.

50 Ibid., p. 116.

51 Sarah van Gelder, *This Changes Everything*, Berret–Koeler, San Francisco, CA, 2011, p. 1.

52 *Occupy Cork*, issue 3, 2011, p. 11.

53 María Clemencia Ramírez, 'The Politics of Recognition and Citizenship', in Boaventura de Sousa Santos (ed.), *Democratizing Democracy*, Verso, London, 2007, p. 238.

54 Max Weber, *Economy and Society* [1919], trans. Ephraim Fischoff et al., ed. Guenther Roth and Claus Wittich, University of California Press, Berkeley, CA, 1968.

55 Barber, *Strong Democracy*.

56 Fintan O'Toole, *Enough is Enough: How to Build a New Republic*, Faber and Faber, London, 2010, p. 21.

57 Linda Connolly and Niamh Hourigan, *Social Movements and Ireland*, Manchester University Press, 2006.

58 Peadar Murphy and Mary P. Murphy, *Towards a Second Republic*, Pluto, London, 2011, pp. 217–18.

Index

pluralism, 38–9, 82, 98, 148
Poland, 18
police, 90, 123, 126, 132, 138, 192, 197
policy-making, 75, 85, 179
populism, 65–6, 74, 91, 127, 173, 175–6, 178
Portugal, 180
postmodernity, 143, 145, 153
poverty, 17, 34
power, dispersal of, 60
powers, separation of, 12, 91, 118, 121, 151, 165
privatisation, 71
Provisional IRA, 29
Prugh, Thomas, 147
public services, 79
public spending, cuts in, 79
public good, *see* common good
public virtue, *see* civic virtue
Putin, Vladimir, 143

Quinn, Rúairi, 108

Raftery, Mary, 42
Ragan, Michael, 117
Ralahine community, 141
Rawls, John, 92, 98, 103, 105, 107
Reagan, Ronald, 74
Rehn, Olli, 88
religious denominational schools, 95, 99–100, 108–14
religious identity, 93, 95, 99
religious insignia, 93, 99
Renaissance, *see* Italian Renaissance thought
Renan, Ernest, 10–11, 32, 34

representation, 57, 91, 118, 167, 183–4
Republic of Ireland Act (1948), 17, 69
Republican Party (US), 48–9
Revenue Commissioners, 127
Robespierre, Maximilien, 32
Rockefeller, David, 70
Roe v. Wade (1973), 122
Roman Catholic Church, 25, 27, 33, 37–9, 41–3, 93, 108, 110, 118, 149–51
Rome, Classical, 18, 56, 60, 89, 97
Rousseau, Jean-Jacques, 20–22, 24–5, 56
Russell, Bertrand, 184
Russell, George, 150
Russia, 143
Ryan report (2009), 43, 151
Ryan v. Attorney General (1965), 119–120

St Paul's Cathedral, London, 161
Saint-Simon, Henri de, 141
salience transfer, 83
Samaras, Antonio, 88
Saussure, Ferdinand de, 187
Scottish Common Sense, 138
'Sean Van Vocht', 5–7
Seanad Éireann (upper house), 62, 83, 86, 126, 164
Second Republic movement, 164–5
self-government, 57, 59, 60, 62–3, 65
self-interest, 32, 40–41, 58, 61, 66, 69, 96–7

ff

Faber and Faber is one of the great independent publishing houses. We were established in 1929 by Geoffrey Faber with T. S. Eliot as one of our first editors. We are proud to publish award-winning fiction and non-fiction, as well as an unrivalled list of poets and playwrights. Among our list of writers we have five Booker Prize winners and twelve Nobel Laureates, and we continue to seek out the most exciting and innovative writers at work today.

Find out more about our authors and books
faber.co.uk

Read our blog for insight and opinion on books and the arts
thethoughtfox.co.uk

Follow news and conversation
twitter.com/faberbooks

Watch readings and interviews
youtube.com/faberandfaber

Connect with other readers
facebook.com/faberandfaber

Explore our archive
flickr.com/faberandfaber